Also from Westphalia Press

WESTPHALIAPRESS.ORG

HISTORY OF THE WORSHIPFUL COMPANY OF GLAZIERS

Westphalia Press
An imprint of Policy Studies Organization
1527 New Hampshire Ave., NW
Washington, D.C. 20036
INFO@IPSONET.ORG

ISBN-13: 978-1-63391-216-8
ISBN-10: 1633912167

Cover design by Taillefer Long at Illuminated Stories:
WWW.ILLUMINATEDSTORIES.COM

Daniel Gutierrez-Sandoval, Executive Director
PSO and Westphalia Press

Updated material and comments on this edition
can be found at the Westphalia Press website:
WWW.WESTPHALIAPRESS.ORG

HISTORY OF THE WORSHIPFUL COMPANY OF GLAZIERS OF THE CITY OF LONDON

OTHERWISE THE COMPANY OF GLAZIERS AND PAINTERS OF GLASS

BY CHARLES HENRY ASHDOWN

WESTPHALIA PRESS

AN IMPRINT OF POLICY STUDIES ORGANIZATION

History of the
Worshipful Company of Glaziers
of the City of London,
otherwise the Company of
Glaziers and Painters of Glass

BY

CHARLES HENRY ASHDOWN, F.R.G.S.

(Hon. Sec. Herts. Archæological Soc.; General Editor "Home Antiquary Series";
Author of "Arms and Armour," "British Castles," etc.)

With Contributory Notes by
PERCY W. BERRIMAN TIPPETTS,
Clerk and Solicitor to the Company.

A COPY OF THIS BOOK IS
PRESENTED BY
MASTER GEORGE PAGET WALFORD
TO EACH MEMBER OF
THE WORSHIPFUL COMPANY OF GLAZIERS
AS A TOKEN OF HIS AFFECTION, ESTEEM AND REGARD,
AND ALSO OF HIS KEEN APPRECIATION OF THE
HONOUR THE COMPANY HAS SHOWN HIM
IN ELECTING HIM TO BE MASTER
DURING THE YEARS
1903–1904; 1916–1917; 1917–1918; 1918–1919.

CONTENTS.

———

ILLUSTRATIONS.

FOREWORD.

———

The compilation of the first History issued by the GLAZIERS' COMPANY OF LONDON has been a labour of considerable interest, not only on account of the subject matter being necessarily entirely new, but also by reason of the essentially human interest pervading the narrative. Although the mediaeval part may prove attractive by its originality, possibly that portion dealing with the troublous times preceding the grant of a Charter may rival it in the minds of many of those for whom these pages are written.

CHARLES H. ASHDOWN.

ST. ALBANS.

———

My thanks are due and are hereby gratefully tendered to the following for kind help:—Sir John Wrench Towse, Clerk to the Worshipful Company of Fishmongers; Sir John Bell, Town Clerk of London; Bernard Kettle, Esq., Guildhall Librarian; Edgar T. A. Wigram, Esq., B.A., A.R.I.B.A.; the Court of Assistants of the Glaziers' Company of London.

HISTORY OF THE
WORSHIPFUL COMPANY OF GLAZIERS
OTHERWISE THE
GLAZIERS AND PAINTERS OF GLASS.

CHAPTER I.

THE ORIGIN, RISE, AND PROGRESS OF THE MEDIAEVAL GUILDS OF ENGLAND.

THE origin, rise and progress of the great Guilds of England form a chapter in the mercantile history of our nation which is only equalled in interest by those dealing with the military and naval aspects, while the triumphs achieved by commercial enterprise have indubitably surpassed in a large number of cases the material advantages accruing from campaigns on land and sea. It will be our pleasant task to trace the progress of these great communities from their inception to the proud position which, so far as the London Companies are concerned, they occupy at the present time.

The word " Guild " is derived from the Anglo-Saxon " gild," meaning " gold," although some authorities assert that the original meaning of the A-S. word was a " feast." If so, the words " company " (from *cum pane, i.e.,* with bread) and " guild " both refer to festivity.

The Craft Guilds of the Middle Ages were composed of communities of men bound together by a common object, namely, the furtherance and protection of the particular craft or mystery by which their livelihood was obtained. There is no doubt that each mystery in earlier times was confined to the members of one particular family who handed down the secrets of the craft to their descendants ; when, however, the latter were unable to deal with increase of trade, then carefully-chosen persons were selected and necessary oaths were administered to them with a view to the preservation of the essential *minutiae* of the craft.   The oaths thus taken, and the penalties imposed in the event of violation, may appear at the present day to be out of all proportion to the pursuit of a calling, but in the absence of protective measures by the State and other restrictions upon imports and production they were the only alternatives practicable under the prevailing circumstances.

The domestic feeling once introduced permeated the guild, and from the earliest times in the 13th century we find the institution of family devotion perpetuated by the appointment of a chaplain.   All meetings of the community commenced with divine worship, while the household charity and benevolence, doubtless lacking discrimination and guiding rules, were regulated by definite areas of almsgiving and assistance.   This feeling, in spite of the vicissitudes to which the London City Companies have been subjected during the passing centuries, remains paramount to the present day, and the benevolent attitude of the Fraternities to deserving institutions has passed into a proverb.   It is true that a relapse occurred shortly after the commencement of the Renaissance, when the greed of gold, fed by overwhelming prosperity, choked the sources whence the fount of almsgiving had flowed ; it was, however, only temporary, and one may safely assert that the general trend of the Guilds' aims and objects from the very first inception have been essentially eleemosynarian.

The Guilds of England came into prominence in that part of the Norman Period when the country was gradually recovering from the destruction wrought during the earlier years of the Conquest, and were stimulated by the large influx of foreigners of all descriptions who flocked into the country, bringing with them ideas of progress and energetic pursuit of commerce hitherto unknown to the English trader ; while the constant intercourse with Normandy, and the numerous family relations of the Conqueror's descendants, led to more extensive travel and enterprise in commerce than had hitherto been known.   Fruitful ground was thus provided for the encouragement of Merchant Guilds and Craft Guilds and in nearly every trade the latter were

1918

Upper Warden:
SIR HARRY SEYMOUR FOSTER, J.P., H.M.L., D.L., *ex-Sheriff of London*

formed in all towns of the Kingdom. The right of making their own rules and regulations for the better ordering of the Guild they bought from their respective Municipalities or from the Sovereign, and rapidly acquired a degree of importance commensurate with the power they wielded in swaying the destinies of the nation.

The procedure necessary to procure membership of a Craft Guild was of a nature singularly familiar to the liveryman of the present day. The youth was bound apprentice to the Master-Craftsman for a term of years to learn the mystery of the trade, and when he had completed the necessary time of training became a free journeyman (Fr. journée " a day's work," and no connection with travelling as generally understood) carrying on with the right to serve any master who required his services. When he acquired sufficient capital to commence work for himself he submitted his master-piece to the Guild, paid his entrance fee, and appeared thenceforward upon the rolls as a master-craftsman.

The Guild Feast was generally an annual celebration to which the members came habited in the appropriate livery of the Company ; elections to offices were made at this assembly, together with grants to those in need of help. Women were enrolled as members of a Guild as well as men. The Merchant Guilds were necessarily of a higher social class than the Craft Guilds, and at times showed intolerance of the latter ; the artisans, however, eventually overcame the opposition and jealousy and were often successful even in forcing their will upon the Corporations. Thus from 1262 to 1265 Thomas Thomasson was Mayor of London by sheer force of man power among the Guilds, and in 1272 they insisted on having Walter Harvey in the same capacity in spite of the Aldermen and Council.

It would be of interest to know where the Guild of Glaziers and Painters of Glass were first located in the City of London, since nearly every Company had its members living in the same locality where the craft was practised. This domestic system is apparent even in the present day, since we have examples of small masters employing assistants and all living under one roof in Whitechapel, where tailoring and shoemaking are carried on ; also exemplifications in the silk weaving at Bethnal Green and the cabinet-making of Shoreditch. In the cutlery trade of Sheffield similar conditions prevail, likewise nail-making of the Black Country, the straw plait of Bedford and Luton, the lace of Nottingham, etc.

In London we find that the Clothiers frequented Cornhill, the Smiths and Tanners, Holborn, and the Braziers, Lothbury. The Pepperers, *i.e.*, Grocers, occupied Soper's Lane (or Queen Street); the Tailors were at Coleman Street; the Drapers, Candlewick Street; Goldsmiths, Westcheap; Vintners, the Vintry; Lawyers and Writers at Chancery Lane; Butchers in S. Nicholas' Shambles and Eastcheap. The great market was Cheapside; the one devoted to Cattle was Smithfield; along the riverside the Fishmongers' stalls were found, and the pork shops were in Eastcheap.

The feelings of brotherhood and mutual help and esteem engendered by the Guilds were among the most precious virtues fostered in the primitive community; but perhaps the dignity of being a member of an Honourable Company produced more tangible results than any other. It placed a commercial man upon a distinctly high level which possibly he has not attained since; the doctrine of the " Dignity of Labour " never had such stout henchmen upholding it as it had at the hands of the mediaeval artisan and trader.

He lived at a time when occupation in commercial pursuits was not considered derogatory to, or incompatible with, dignity, for the upper classes themselves were engaged in its prosecution in various forms. The great Lords of the Manor disposed of the produce of their lands in the open cheapings, and purchased the necessaries of life at the same time. Knights and nobles, abbots and priests, made a business of selling the harvests of their lands, monastic estates, or glebes; royalty itself did not disdain to engage in the traffic, but had ships trading with foreign countries, Edward IV being by no means unique in this respect. The nobleman with dependent sons allocated vocations to each impartially; one was to succeed him; another to enter the military service; the law claimed a third and the Church a fourth, while commerce was perhaps the fortune of the remainder. Thus a Chandos might have a master Mercer for a brother, a Grossetête be proud of his affinity with a Glazier's apprentice. Caste prejudices were inevitably softened and artificial barriers broken down, for the leading men of the commercial classes stood upon the same level as those of other professions. They were often ennobled, often did noteworthy actions bringing renown and credit to the State, and Arteveldes could be found in England as well as in Ghent.

Not only by land but by sea merchants fiercely upheld the dignity of their calling. Did not John Philpot, of London Town, in 1377, collect a number of vessels, place 1,000 armed men upon them, and sail for the North, where in a short space of time he routed a piratical force of marauders and seized 15 ships laden with wine ? It is true that the proceeding was considered high-handed by a peace-at-any-price section of the community, and that he was summoned before the London Council upon his return; his spirited answer fortunately has been preserved for us, and convincingly shows the patriotism, enterprise, and energy which characterised the mediaeval trader. " I did not expose myself, my money and my men to the dangers of the sea that I might deprive you and your colleagues of your knightly fame, nor that I might win any for myself; I went in pity for the misery of the people and the country, which, from being a noble realm with dominion over other nations, has, through your supineness, become exposed to the ravages of the vilest race, and I exposed myself and my property for the safety and deliverance of my country."

There are, no doubt, members of the community who, even in the present day of intelligent estimation and enlargement of ideas, " look down " upon the man engaged in trade, but the failing is only a late survival of the bad old mid-Victorian days when the accepted definition of a gentleman was " one who did nothing." We are devoutly thankful that no Thackeray is needed at the present time, and that those unworthy feelings are dying a well-merited death. The great merchant princes of to-day had their prototypes in mediaeval times and, similarly, lent a dignity to all connected with them. Often consulted upon affairs of State, they are, and were, ennobling the calling to which they belong.

Some of the names of Merchant Princes handed down from the Middle Ages are even now household words. The de la Poles of Hull, for example, whose progenitor, a merchant of the neighbouring port of Ravensern, practically laid the foundation of the prosperity of Hull by his wisdom, energy and enterprise; he eventually rose to be the chief merchant in England, honoured by Edward III, while his son was ennobled by Richard II with the title of Earl of Suffolk. The Cannynges of Bristol, Sir John Crosby of London, and also Sir Richard Whittington, are familiar names. Most of the great mediaeval traders have left substantial evidences of their munificence by the founding of churches, like St. Mary Redcliffe, while many of their counterfeit presentments are preserved to us in the form of monumental brasses like those of Walsoken and Robert Braunche at Lynn, and the great wool-kings of Northleach.

The adoption by the Guilds of a dress similar to that of the monastic orders gave to the Fraternities a semi-ecclesiastical tone, quite in accordance with their avowed principles and objects; while the choice of a Saint to whose protection the welfare of the Company was confided served to accentuate their religious position. The Saint selected was symbolical of the craft, if possible, thus the Fishmongers chose St. Peter. Altars to the Patron Saint were founded; and gorgeous processions of liveried members, with dignitaries of the Church in pontificals, were of common occurrence before the Reformation. Liveries are definitely mentioned for the first time when Edward I married his second wife, Margaret, sister of Philip IV, King of France, in 1299, at Canterbury. The Guilds then mustered upon horseback to the number of six hundred, clad in one livery of red and white and bearing, in embroidery upon their sleeves, the cognizances of their mysteries (Fr. métier, or mestier, a trade or occupation). The capuchon, or hood, was apparently an indispensable adjunct of the livery since it figures in descriptions of the dress for many centuries, even after that head-dress had been generally discarded by the laity. Thus, in the time of Henry VI and Edward IV hoods were worn instead of the prevailing chaperons and roundels.

Chaucer thus refers to the dress of the Guildsman, and also, incidentally, to his accredited position :—

> An Haberdasher and a Carpenter,
> A Webbe, a Deyer, and a Tapiser,
> Were all y-clothed in liverie,
> Of a solempne and grete Fraternite.

The London Companies are a unique survival of the vanished Guilds which at one time were customary in all English mediaeval towns ; if the place happened to be small then various crafts were included under one denomination, a common hall serving for the whole. Thus in St. Albans, in 1634, there were four companies which embraced all the others; the Mercers, for example, included twenty-nine fraternities amongst whom we find the local Glaziers' Company.

In the majority of European countries to-day the great trading companies of mediaeval origin are non-existent, and in England they remain practically only in the metropolis, and there under such altered conditions as to have little resemblance to their original prototypes. The reason for this wide elimination may almost be termed the evolution of a universal law which affects nations and communities alike—they fall apart after a time by reason of their own unwieldiness. In some cases internal dissensions formed no mean part in causing disintegration of the Craft Guilds, and the crown had, at times, to undertake the settlement of internecine disputes.

But probably the chief cause was the rise of the capitalists, whereby the old fellowship and camaraderie engendered by master and man working together at the same bench was abolished, and the commencement of mutual distrust ensued. The capitalists became the heads of the guilds and monopolised the power ; their positions gradually evolved into hereditary rights, and communism sank into the background. Persons were admitted to the fraternities who had nothing in common with the mystery concerned ; by payments of certain sums of money one could obtain the privileges of practically any Guild. These innovations caused bitterness of feeling, litigation ensued at times and the subsequent awards tended in not a few cases to deepen and accentuate the indignation of the older members. A dispute in the Goldsmiths' Company, in 1539, has become historical. Thus members of Companies, no longer held together by mutual brotherhood and self-interest, gradually died out, and Guilds became extinct.

Another reason for the decay was the fact that the wealth owned by the Guilds, and their domination by town corporations, rendered them peculiarly liable to irregular taxation and spoliation by successive Governments, both municipal and imperial,—the need of money by local authorities or by the State being always considered sufficient justification for coercing the Companies. The Commonwealth period had much to do with the extinction of Guilds, for the Companies were forced to contribute large sums to the national exchequer, chiefly to pay the expenses of the war. There was also a City custom whereby at one time they were bound to lend money to the municipality to purchase corn and fuel for the poor in times of scarcity.

So far as the City Companies were concerned, the Great Fire of London caused the ruin of many. Their Halls, Almshouses and house property were destroyed in a number of instances, and by being unable to raise the necessary sums for re-building, the Guilds fell into desuetude. The colonisation of Ulster in the reign of James I was also a cause of decay to the Guilds, for the Companies were compelled to purchase and undertake the settlement of large tracts of land in the County of Londonderry (*vide* extracts from Minutes of the Glaziers' Company of January 29th, 1701).

The survival of those that remain has probably been more influenced and safeguarded by their wealth, social distinction, and strength of vested interest than by any other reason, consequently any Government intent upon spoliation turned aside to attack less formidable opponents. The Royal Commission of 1880 has become a welcome safeguard of their rights, and no doubt whatever can be entertained that so long as the existing Companies proceed upon the excellent lines now pursued of encouraging every good work tending to foster education, social science, and human progress in general, combined with that liberality which ennobles the giver without degrading the recipient, so long will they flourish and remain a valuable asset to the Empire.

CHAPTER II.

ORIGIN AND RISE OF THE WORSHIPFUL COMPANY OF GLAZIERS
AND PAINTERS OF GLASS.

THE process of staining glass in various colours was well known to the Ancients, but the art of glass painting belongs to the mediaeval period, and is essentially a product of Christian civilisation and artistic evolution. Modern research appears to lead to the conclusion that as early as the 7th century A.D., painted glass was known upon the Continent, the French claiming the honour of the invention. Gregory of Tours, who died in 595, speaks of windows of coloured glass, while plain glass was brought over to England by Benedict Biscop, the Abbot of Wearmouth, in 674. In 709, Wilfred, Bishop of York, invited glass workers from France to settle in England, and when glass painting was revived, or more probably introduced, during the 10th century, the method of preparing it was described by the monk Theophilus.

Glass windows, however, were of great rarity during the Saxon period ; the embrasures in church walls for admitting light and air were usually only filled by crossed strings to exclude birds; oiled parchment, however, was occasionally used. During the Norman period the use of glass in churches and also in the better class of domestic buildings began slowly to come into use, but it was not until the early English period, which commenced in the 12th century, that stained glass made its appearance. Probably none of that early date remains, but examples of 13th century glass are to be found in England.

The lead work of the earlier examples of glass windows in England was of a very broad and strong nature, massiveness being its chief characteristic ; at the Renaissance it became lighter in appearance although possessing the same strength, in consequence of the lead being made narrower and thicker with a rounded surface upon the exterior.   Early mediaeval saddle-bars often followed the salient lines of the subject depicted in the window, and thus obviated the unsightly crossing of the features by horizontal lines.   As we pen these words a portion of the magnificent rose window of the south transept of Ypres cathedral lies upon the table ; the leading is of the broad variety, the quarries very small and a quarter of an inch or more in thickness ; the latter measurement varies, however, and is an exemplification of the theory that modern glass with uniform thickness, freedom from bubbles and accidental variations of opacity can never vie with the mediaeval variety in richness and softness of tone.   The window itself, as a window, is alas ! no more, and the world is the poorer for the loss.

The effect of stained glass windows upon ecclesiastical edifices cannot be over-estimated.   They produce a feeling of repose and rich contentment which only those who have viewed the far-famed Seven Sisters can appreciate, while the effect upon the artistic and spiritual senses of the glorious display in St. Peter Mancroft, or the subtle harmonies of St. Mary's, Shrewsbury, are beyond the power of the pen to describe.

It may safely be asserted that while in many ecclesiastical edifices there are features we would willingly like to see removed, it is very seldom that a stained glass window forms one of them.   The rose window in the south transept of Westminster for a time, unfortunately, fell under this category, but, since the insertion of new glass, general satisfaction has prevailed.

With regard to leaded lights, the great revival of the art during the past twenty-five years is a conclusive answer to any question as to whether the people of England recognise their beauty.   Few that have sat behind them fail to appreciate the coolness, actual or imaginary, which seems inseparable from their nature ; while their presence, if only in a late Renaissance edifice, generally evokes a laudatory comment from the observer.

A comparatively new building acquires an added charm from their presence, and even when surrounded by crass modernity their influence is felt.   Who that has traversed a crowded thoroughfare, not a Sabbath day's journey from Old Bond Street, has failed to notice the cool, inviting entrance to a perfume establishment ; has not lingered long in the soft diffused daylight of the interior, and then reluctantly stepped out once more into the blazing heat of a cloudless sun.

The masters of the craft of leaded-window making are, however, not always successful in their manipulation of the ancient art, for a cathedral exists in the Home Counties which boasts of a window with five lancets, the centre one being the tallest in England. The window was filled with leaded glass not two decades since, and a few years afterwards began shedding quarries indiscriminately and impartially within and without the sacred edifice, while a series of undulations, interesting but dangerous, appeared upon the erstwhile plane surface. A sum of nearly £250 was expended before it could be rendered safe.

It is somewhat strange that the early production in England of iron and also of glass should have flourished in a district where at the present time these industries are extinct, namely, the Weald of Surrey and Sussex. The grand old oak forests once covering that district and revelling in the tenacious wealden clay, are now no more, except in meagre patches, and this denudation was brought about by the presence of the manufactures mentioned. Glass producers appear to have settled about 1230 at Chiddingfold on the borders of Surrey and Sussex, attracted doubtless by the abundance of fuel. They seem to have flourished, for about a century afterwards, in 1350, we learn that John Alemayen, residing at Chiddingfold—whose name engenders a suspicion that he was of German origin—supplied flat, colourless window glass for glazing purposes to St. Stephen's Chapel at Westminster, and also for St. George's Chapel, Windsor.

A record is extant that John Glasewirth, a Staffordshire glass worker, came to reside at Kirdford, a village in Sussex between Petworth and Chiddingfold, in 1318. English glass, however, during the early part of the 15th century, did not bear a very exalted reputation, since in 1447, when the Beauchamp Chapel at St. Mary's, Warwick, was to be glazed, the contractor bound himself under penalties not to use English flat glass.

Later, however, the reaction occurred, and in 1487, English glass for glazing purposes was preferred to Normandy, Dutch, and even to Venetian glass. During the first half of the 16th century the industry did not flourish, and it was reserved for the reigns of King Henry VIII and Queen Elizabeth to witness the great revival in the art and mystery of the making of glass.   In 1565, on August 7th, Armagill Wade in writing to Sir William Cecil, Secretary of State, respecting the progress of the manufacture of glass under the control of Cornelius de Lannoy, made a special reference to the clumsiness of English glassmakers.

In 1567, August 12th, the Domestic State Papers of the Reign of Queen Elizabeth refer to articles made between the Queen and Anthony Becker, alias Dobin, and John Carre.   The latter was a native of Antwerp and had erected furnaces in Surrey and Sussex (possibly at Chiddingfold and Kirdford) for glass making.   He proposed to the Queen to make glass such as was used in France and Lorraine.   This probably meant the manufacture of discs or circles, the method pursued in Normandy, from which the quarries could be cut, and also, in addition, the process of making glass in the form of cylinders, as in Lorraine, which were afterwards cut down the sides, or split, re-heated and flattened out.   Carre's works subsequently spread into Hampshire and the adjacent counties, eventually reaching Northumberland and penetrating even into Scotland and Ireland.

In 1568 a request was made by " Anthony Becque " and " J. Quarre " (the Becker and Carre already mentioned), Glassmakers to the Queen, to allow them to cut wood, make charcoal, etc., in Windsor Great Park and convey it thence.   Whether the permission was granted does not appear.   The firm did not proceed without a certain amount of opposition, for, in 1574, Bishop R. Coortesse, of Chichester, speaks of a combination "to rob the Frenchmen who make glasse," and in 1584 a man named Nicholas Moore applied to the Queen for a license to make glass within her realm.   Moore was not the only person who applied thus, for we find that as early as July, 1567, Carre wrote to Cecil as follows :—

" I have erected two glass houses at Fernefol, in Sussex, for Normandy and Loraine glass by Her Majesty's Licence, and one in London by leave of the Lord Mayor and Aldermen for crystal glass (possibly at Newgate) ; also brought over workmen at my own great cost and to benefit of the Kingdom, on sending for Soda from Spain, that of London not being good.   Yet I hear that another is likely to have the privilege of making glass, which would ruin me and prevent my paying you and Her Majesty what I owe you. Pray remember the promise you made me in Oxfordshire that I should have the advantage ; let this be prevented and let me have the patent for 21 years."

A reference to painted glass occurs in the State Paper under date 1591, " Sir John Harte, Governor, and the Russia Company to Christopher Holme Agent. The eight stories in Glass for the Ste Twerdia are not ready yet."

The late revival of leaded lights has also conduced to the re-introduction of the hinged casement, a lineal descendant of the ancient wooden shutter. The glass itself in these modern times is generally the least expensive part of the whole window, but we have only to go back to the Tudor Period to discover the reverse. For example, during the reign of Queen Elizabeth, and in the immediately preceding years, the cost of glass was so high and prohibitive that windows of that material could be afforded only by the opulent.

When, however, the price came within reasonable reach of the average purse, windows became large, and as numerous as possible for the purpose of display ; this formed a marked feature of late-Perpendicular architecture for
" Hardwick Hall,
More glass than wall,"
is an old adage, and this characteristic lasted until the window tax of 1753 effectually curbed it. Even, however, with the advent of cheaper glass it was the custom for many of the great people to carry with them in their coaches when travelling from one of their mansions to another, the precious panes of glass, so that one set might do for several houses, or else to have it removed and stored in safety until their return.

The excessive cost of glass was indubitably enhanced by the pernicious system of granting monopolies which, coming into existence in the time of King Henry VIII, grew to abnormal proportions under Elizabeth and James I, and was not by any means stopped even when the Act of 1623 made all monopolies illegal. The granting to favourites and wealthy persons the sole right of making and selling a certain article was the method by which post-mediaeval monarchs filled their ever-empty purses, and compensated their depleted exchequers for the abolition of Forced Loans and other atrocities which had hitherto fulfilled the same purpose. These privileges, the forerunners of the patent rights of the present time, might or might not be used for the good of the community by the grantee; in so many cases, however, were patents abused that the system became a burden and hindrance to the progress of the nation.

It was in consequence of a spirited fight by the Glaziers' Guild against one of the monopolies granted by Elizabeth that they obtained their Charter of Incorporation.   Doubtless the effect of other monopolies was instrumental in aiding their decision, not the least being the all-pervading want of a proper regal copper coinage, the grant of making which to outsiders resulted finally in a gigantic national scandal, and the production of the Harrington farthings which were so thin and light that they could easily be blown off the palm of the hand.

From certain indications which have come to our knowledge a belief prevails among many that a City Company springs into existence when its Charter of Incorporation is granted.   This has been the case in a few instances it is true, but with regard to the great majority of Companies the granting of a Charter has been but an incident in its career, and may be compared with marriage in the life of a man, not synchronising in fact with any fixed part of his life and sometimes not occurring at all.   The Guilds from which some Companies have sprung may possibly have attained greater eminence individually before their incorporation than they have realised since, and the petition for a charter sprang in most cases, like that of the Glaziers, from a desire to redress evils, or from a wish to still further foster their particular spheres of usefulness.

These remarks have been made with a view to combat any idea on the part of members of the Glaziers' Company that the importance of the Fraternity must be judged from its action since the time of Charles I, when the Charter was granted, down to the present period ; records tend to show, if not to prove conclusively, that centuries before that event the Brotherhood was doing good and useful work.

CHAPTER III.

ORIGIN AND RISE OF THE WORSHIPFUL COMPANY OF GLAZIERS
AND PAINTERS OF GLASS—*continued.*

TO a certain extent window glass may be classed as a luxury, inasmuch as our forefathers practically did without it during the Saxon and Norman periods. Naturally, therefore, a record-searcher would not expect to meet with the term "glazier" as early as that of, say, "mercer," "cordwainer," or of any similar person dealing in necessities. This has been borne out in compiling the present book. The name of the earliest glazier unearthed is that of Thomas le Verer,* of Oxford, 1236, which occurs in the Close Rolls for the years 1234 to 1237, preserved in the Record Office. In a Patent Roll of Henry III a Safe Conduct until the Purification is granted to John le Verrer, a Friar Preacher, October 12th, 1265, and on June 22nd, 1268, a pardon was granted to Guy le Verrer, of the County of Essex, by mainprise of John Saunzcer and Robert le Depoining of Lancaster.

In 1279, May 15th, Adam le Verrer was nominated his attorney by John de Peteshull, who was going beyond the seas, and John le Verrer is mentioned in connection with Canterbury on 23rd July, 1305, in the Patent Rolls, 33 Edward I. Again, in 1281, December 5th (9 Edward I), in a Commission of Oyer and Terminer, on the complaints of John de Cleykarwell and Matilda, his wife, that whereas they had lately gone out for a walk at Admodesham, Co. Bucks, William le Verrer and eight others had assaulted them so that their lives were despaired of. William le Verrer, on November 8th, 1303,

---

* The term "Vitreur" for glazier is derived from *Vitrearius* (Lat.) a maker of glass ; it is abbreviated to *vitrarii* in some mediaeval petitions. Similarly the glaziers are referred to as *verrurs, verrers,* and *verres* (Fr. *verre,* glass), and possibly the beaders whose names occur in the early MSS. were glaziers. It is more than possible that members of the Glaziers' Company may search original records with a view to ascertaining the traces, if any, the Guild has left on English history before the reign of Edward III ; and, if so, they should bear the above clues in mind. The Author of this book or the Clerk of the Company will be pleased to hear of any finds of this nature with a view to their incorporation in future issues.

complained that the Prior of Wenlock, the Parson of Stoke Church, the Pastor of Doddington, and others entered his manor, stole a dozen cows and carried away corn, etc., while another William le Verrur, on May 26th, 1305, was accused by the Prior of the Friar Preachers of entering his bounds with a large crowd, felling trees, carrying away the gates and committing other misdemeanours. After the beginning of the fourteenth century the number of Verrers increases considerably in the records.

The earliest mention, so far discovered, of the Company of Glaziers occurs in a list of names compiled in December, 1328, the second year of the reign of Edward III, being the

" Names of those Elected and Sworn in divers Misteries of London
for the Government and Instruction of the same, viz. :—

> *Glasyrs*   John Husbonde, *Master.*
> Alan Gille, *Warden.*
> Walter Neel.
> John de Wrotham.
> Richard de Reynham.
> Hamo le Barber.
> John atte Loka.
> John Spray.
> John de Warefield.

The first two names in most of the mediaeval lists of City Companies are those of the Master and Senior Warden, and it is suggested that this list follows the same practice. It is to be found in the Guildhall Records of the City of London, Letter Book E. fo. 190.

The Glaziers' Guild is among those that were thoroughly reorganised in the time of King Edward III, who took a keen interest in the welfare of the City Companies, even proceeding so far as to become a Member of one. All the Companies and Guilds up to that period had existed only on sufferance.

The rearrangement referred to consisted for one thing in defining the livery which should distinguish the Companies, but principally in revising the laws and ordinances by which they were governed, discarding those that were obsolete and introducing necessary new regulations more in accordance with the spirit of the times. Under the latter category those advanced by the Glaziers' Guild in that reign, which we have been fortunate enough to discover, are of interest, not only because of their antiquity, but also as showing the nature of the grievances which had prevailed among the fraternity in former years, and the anxiety manifested to have them redressed.

The original petition is couched in Old French, since that language was in general use at the Law Courts at the time of King Edward III, and was also the speech prevailing in polite society :—

(1364-5. 28 February.)

Petition of the good folk " Verrers" (La ordinance de " Verres ") of the City to the Mayor and Aldermen that certain ordinances (poyntz) may be allowed for the good of the mistery, to the following effect :

First, that if any stranger come to the City and desires to use the said mistery as a master, the good folk elected and sworn to rule the said mistery shall come to the Mayor and Aldermen and inform them of the name of such person, and the Mayor and Aldermen shall cause him to appear before them, and he shall be examined by good folk of the mistery to see if he be fit and sufficiently informed to use the mistery and of good character to remain in the City.

Also that no one entice servants or journeymen (lowys)* from their master.

Also that if any servant who has lawfully served his master fall sick or become poor he shall be maintained (trove)† by the men of the mistery.

Also that any servant who does wrong and refuses to submit to the good folk of the mistery shall be brought before the Mayor and Aldermen to be punished.

Also that no one shall take apprentice or keep open shop unless he be free of the City nor shall he take journeyman or servant unless proved and found by the masters of the mistery to know his craft, and if any journeyman be found ignorant of his craft, he shall be put out of it unless he be willing to become an apprentice to learn his craft.

Also that if any of the mistery be found working within the Franchise contrary to the above ordinance, his work shall be forfeited and he shall pay 20s. to the mistery.

Also that if any one be found making false work, the work shall be carried to the Mayor and Aldermen and there shall be judged by the masters of the craft.

Also if any journeyman or servant remove work without permission of his master, so as to withdraw profit from his master, he shall pay 40s. to the Commonalty and 20s. to the mistery.

---

* *Louer* (O.F.), to hire one's self to another.
† *Trouver* (Fr.), to find. The expression " everything found " is of a like character.

It will be noted that the Ordinances are particularly directed against the grievances which were paramount during the Middle Ages in labour questions, namely, the influx of foreigners professing the same craft, and the employment of unskilled labour.   The remedy suggested is at all times the same, and was probably efficacious—the *sine qua non* that the workman should be a Freeman of the City and also that he should have served an apprenticeship to the craft he professed.

The Freedom of the City was no empty honour as erroneously supposed by those non-versed in the matter, inasmuch as a man was not at liberty to open a place of business, to enter upon retail trade, or even to live in the City and its confines for any lengthy period without it.   It carried with it the privilege of trading both wholesale and retail with fellow citizens and with strangers, of sending or taking goods wherever he chose, and of entering any town without being mulcted in murage, or the dues exacted by corporations upon goods entering their city walls.   A Freeman of the City of London could with a few minor exceptions also claim exemption from the legal jurisdiction of ultra-mural Courts of Law, and upon his demise his relatives could claim the return of his burial expenses in the event of civic funeral honours not being accorded him.

When this book was projected a strong and justifiable supposition existed that in mediaeval times the " Glaziers and Painters of Glass " and the " Glass Sellers " formed one and the same Guild, by reason of their dealing with the same substance, and that research would disclose the period when bifurcation ensued.   These supposititious premises have now to be negatived, since no evidence whatever has been forthcoming to suggest coalition of the two Companies or even that they existed side by side.   The " Glass Sellers " whose particular functions are defined as " makers and sellers of looking glasses and sellers (not makers) of glasses, bottles, etc.," received their Charter in 1664, and in the History issued by them no reference occurs as to a Guild previously existing, from which they sprang.

That jurisdiction was exercised by the Municipality of London over the Guilds and Companies of the City of London is evidenced by the permission sought to elect certain persons to be Masters and Wardens as the following will show. The terms "Master" and "Warden" are interchangeable, the first named is the master and the second the warden.

Magri vitrear. 1368, May 10 (42 Edward III). This day and year came the Glaziers (vitrarii) before the Mayor and Aldermen, and presented Henry Stannerne and William Papelwyk, glaziers, to the wardens of their mistery, etc.

1373, July 7th. Tuesday before the Feast of Translation of St. Thomas, 47 Edward III, John de Brampton " glasiere," and John Geddynagge, " glasiere," elected Masters of the Mistery of Glaziers, and sworn to rule the said mistery and present defaults, etc.

One of the most attractive and diversified Petitions among the many that have been presented by the Glaziers is that of 1474, in the reign of King Edward IV. It is given here in full, as any attempt to curtail it would involve a loss to our readers of quaint and interesting matter :—

(BOOK L OF CITY OF LONDON LETTER BOOKS.)

A.D. 1474. July 27th, 14th year of reign of K. Edward IV came good men of the Mistery of Glaziers and presented to the Mayor and Aldermen the following petition :—

To þe right honourable lord þe Mair and Thaldremen of þe Citae of London Makely busichan your good lordships and Maistershippes your powere Oratours þe Wardeyns and other good Folkes enfranchesed of and in the Crafte or mystere of Glasiers of þe said Citae. Where in tyme passed when Fremen oonely of the same Citae exercised and used the same craft and mistery for the tyme beyng all man' of werk' concernying the said Craft and Mistere were truely and profitably made and wrought w'oute sleight, fraude or deceite to the pleasur' of Almighty god and þe comon profit of the people of þe Citae aforesaid as by the old werkes of the said Craft and Mistere of old tyme made it may appere more at large unto nowe of late daies certain Foreyn persons as well etrangers as other to þe noumbre of XXVIIjᵉ and more in secrete corners as Chaumbres and oþere private places of þe said Citae and nye thereunto adjoynyng some theym of grete untrueth and subtilte and some for lak of Kunnyong have used and daile use to werk and exercise deceivably and unknownyngly the said craft and Mistere, as it may full evedently appere by divers of their werkes now of late by sundry of þeym so made and set up in divers plaices of the said Citae of whom nor of whose werk the Wardens of the said Craft and Mistere for the tyme beyng in no wise can or may for þe causes aforesaid have any oversight serche or correccion That it wold like your said goode lordship and Maistershippes the premisses considred to do ordeigne enacte and establish for evermore that no maner of persone hereafter straunger nor other in any wise take uppon theym to excercise nor use the said Craft or Mistere wᵗin the said Citae nor the lib'tie þereof except that þeir be Fremen of the said Citae and þereunto enhabled and approved connyngmen in the saim Craft or mystere by the Wardens and ij oþer of the said craft and mystere more expert and hable in the same by the said Wardeins for þᵉ tyme beyng to theym to that entent to be named and chosen And that þᵉ Wardeins of the said Craft and Mistere for the tyme beyng wᵗ an Officer of the saide Citae by the Mair or Chamb'leyn of the same for the tyme beyng thein appoynted and assigned shall move at all tymes hereafter make due serche of al maner of werk enncernyng the said Craft or Mistere to be made wrought or used wᵗin the same Citae or þᵉ lib'tie þereof and that they shall mowe at all tymes hereafter take and brynge afore the Mair or Chamb'lein of the said Citae for the tyme beyng all maner of werk concernynge the said Crafte or Mistere by þeym so taken and not sufficiently made and wrought and the maker þereof The same maker þerefore to be punnyeshed and make fyne after the discrec'ons of the said Mair and Chamber-leyn or oon of them for the tyme beyng. According to their or his dein'ites or deim'ite in that behelf and the laws and Customes of þᵉ said Citae in suche cases of old tymes used wᵗin the Citae aforesaid The oon half þ'eof to be applied to thuse of the Co'ialtie of the same Citae and the oþ'e half þ'eof to thuse of the Co'ialtie and pore people of the said Craft and Mistery And all suche werke or werkes so as is aforesaid by þᵉ said Wardeyns and Officer to be taken deceivably and not sufficiently made and wrought then to be adiugged and det'myned after the discrecions or discrecion laws and customes aforesaid And your said pow'e Orators shall specially pray to Almyghty God for your noble estates theur lives lastyng.

Their petition was granted.

A petition of the Worshipful Company of Glaziers and Painters of Glass presented in the reign of King Henry VIII is worthy of reproduction here as being couched in quaint language and showing forcibly the grievances under which the Fraternity laboured in the Tudor Period through the presence of untrained alien workmen in their midst, and by the variable prices of the different kinds of glass. The preamble is carried to an inordinate length and, like the dragon of Wantley, or a lady's letter, has the sting in its tail (or the postscript). The prices ruling at the time of its inditement are of considerable interest.

23 *Feb. anno* 33 *Henry VIII* (1541-2).

Item. The Bill of petycon [petition] of the Glaziers and also their certyficat concernyng the pryces of glasse of their workmanshyppe of the same were read and fully debated and proyred and the contente of them was fully granted and agreyd by the hole Court commanded by the same to be entred of record.

To the Right Honble the Lord Maiors of the Cytie of London and their ryght Worshippeful maistre-Aldrem^n of ye same Citie   In their most humblewyse brethren and showen unto yours Lordship and maystreships to poore wardeins and cityzens of ye Craft of Glaziers of ye sayde Citie that wherefore mainetaine-ment of yours saide Orators and such as be their apprentyces certain goode ordynances before thys tyme have been devysed and mayd by the poore powers of yours Oratours and allowed by the Honorable Court and have served of use in the same y^t may please youre goode Lordshyp and maystershippes eftsones [forthwith] to satysfie and affirm the said ordynances of youre saide Oratours and that ye will accept the honest Inglelysshemen being goode workemen unto the Libertys of this saide Cytie paying suche reasonable figures for the same to the use of this Cytie as by your saide discrecon shall be thought reasonable no personnes God wylling be yet goode so gave cunnyng working men of this Citye and Libertyes proof that then it may please your good Lordship and maystreshippes to accept such streungers as be good workemen and of honest commendacon as you shall fynde convenyent and in case your good lordshyp and maystreshyppes be not good unto your said orators in their behaulf they shall be shorteley utterley undone and not able to keepe anye craft by reasonne of the great resortte of strengers into thys noble Cytie whereof the mast part of them knowe not theire occupacon.

The certyficate of the Wardens of the Glazyers to the Lord Maior of the Citae of London and hys right Worshyppefull brethren the Ayldremen of the same concernyng the Pryces of all Kyndes of Glasse and how they maye worke by the daye [for] the Worshyppeful cytyzens of this citie and others the Kynge's loveing subjects finding themself meat and drynke and how being burded [boarded] by them that they worke not.

First the said Warden sayen that yett farre above their knowledge and powr to apoint or rate any certein pryces of the Kynde and sorte of glasse for any longer tyme to continue fore them are but sorrye poore men and have but small store thereof in theire own hande or posseson but even as these have made proofe thei report to worshippeful magistrete of thys Cityie that have itte to sell and bye it as goode cheape as thei cause bye there after must their neede sell so that the plentie or scarcytie in the market maketh alway the pryce thereof   **And** theye desyre this Honble Court as thei before have desyred that they may bee ordered from tyme to tyme by the same both for their reasonable safement of the pryces of the said sorte of glasse and the workmanshyppe thereof and also for the preservacon and maintenance of such goode rules and ordynances as heretofore have been devysed and sett fynish by theire poore selves and allowed and confyrmed by this hon^{ble} Court as that their and theire poore fellowshyppe

maye have competent lyving by their occupacon **And** not to be utterly undone
by the grete nombre of Alyons foreine and strengyrs useing their crafte in thys
noble cytie as commonly almost at thys daye as the sayde poore Wardeins and
their felowshyp being fremen of the same citie to their utter undoing of the said
poore felowship of remedie for them be not the son pryded by this said Court
Nevertheless thei said that whensoever they may bye the best Normandie glass
under XX*s* the case then will thei be contented to sell the same for a grote
[groat] the foote so that there may be not above Viij quarrels in the foote
and if there be X quarrels thereof in the foote then for iiij*d* and if there be
xij quarrels thereof to the foote iiij*d*   And as for burgom [Burgundy] glasse
the comon pryce thereof at this tyme being wrought after the most usual sorte
they may aforde it iiij the foote and fflemishe glasse of lyke workmanshyp at
iiij the foote and as for dyse work [daywork] and proofe [piecework] they can
not rate yet for any pryce certaine but even as shall please the byer thereof to
have it wrought either with colours or without and as for their wage they were
fynding themself meate and drynke for viij*d* the day and beinge found the same
by them that their worke with for vj the day.   Thei are very foxie that so
molest and trouble your lordship and maystershyppe with their business but only
that very meede and necessity constraynte them to do Wherefore thei beseche
this Honble Court in the honour of Almyghty god to have pittie upon them and
to ayde and delyver them at this their trouble into the Way of Charitie.

The Petition of the Glaziers in 1541-2 complaining of the great influx of
" foreigners " (by which is meant non-freemen of the City, strangers from
other towns, or Continental workmen) who practised the Glazier's craft without being qualified was not apparently always remembered by the City
Fathers who, as in the following case, when moved by compassion, allowed
these immigrant unskilled workmen to carry out contracts on paying a nomi-
nal fine to the Guild:—

1560. Feb. 13.   *Item* for certain considerations reasonably movying the Court it was
    thys day ordered by the same that the Vardeyns of the Glaziers shalle pinytt
    [permit] the Foreyn [foreigners] that the schirchewayrdens [churchwardens] of
    the psche [parish] church of greyte seynt barthes [Bartholomew's] have lately
    lyved and sett wyndows to ye aforesaid church and to fynishe the same takynge
    xij*d*. of theym for a fyne for thys onne and no more.

The Glaziers in this case did not, however, calmly submit to the violation of
their privileges, but sent in a remembrance to which the following refers :—

Item. 1561. Mr Malory Mr Maynard and Mr Gilberd Aldermen assigned by the Court
    here this day to consider and reforme the Glasiers bill here exhibited and they
    shall mayke good to mayke report thereof with convenient speede.

The "convenient speed" does not appear to have resulted in very strenuous haste since on June 20th, 1566, 8th year of Elizabeth, we note—

Item the Glaziers' Bill or petityon was gave this daye orde and ordeyred that the answere shall be geven before the next court day.

1570. Dec. 30. *Item* It is ordered that all those Companyes that occupye Glasinge not beyinge Free of the Companye of Glasyers shall not keepe any more apprentices than accordynge to an order here taken in this Courte about fyve yeares past for the same.

A search has been made for the order in question but without result.

The following order of Court appears under the date February 1st, 1572 :—

It was ordered and devysed by this Court that itte shall and may be lawful to and for the Wardeyns of the Company of the Glasiers of thys Cytie to make search in home of William Keymes Clothworker useing the occupation of a Glasyere being a Freeman of this Cytie according to their graunte.

1575, Feb. 24. The Aldermen began the examination of certain complaints made by the Wardens and Company of the Glaziers, who ask for power to arrest aliens using the trade of glaziers as other Companies have power to do. They ask that those aliens must become members of the Glaziers' Company.

The Petition is a very lengthy one, and throughout it the Glaziers are referred to as a Company.

1580. The Glasshouse in Newgate.

It was debated in open Court whether the Glass House at Newgate should continue or not, and it was finally decided that it should be discontinued.

1582, June 1. A Caution issued by the Court of Aldermen to the City Companies to pay their rates at this time includes the name of the Glaziers.

1585. Nov. 23. 28th year of Queen Elizabeth. "This day Miles Mason, Glasyer, was admitted into the roome and offyce of Glasyer to the Chamber of this Cytie to have hole exercise to manage the same offyce so long as he shall well and honestly use and behave himself in the execution thereof and not otherwise."

It was evidently judicious on the part of the Council to insert the latter clause *re* behaviour, for we find that a successor of Miles Mason, named William Holly, was discharged from his office of "Glazier to the City" for "grosse and obstinate carriage against the Court," and on September 28th, 1624, Richard Buttler was appointed Holly's successor, doubtless with the same proviso annexed.

Hazlitt states that "Young, glazier to the Queen, lived in Wood Street, Cheapside, and it is said that the head of James IV of Scotland, when his embalmed remains were taken from Shene Monastery after the Dissolution, and cast on a rubbish heap, was secured from the trunk by a workman, and came into Young's possession. The latter kept it for some time, and was struck by its freedom from any offensive odour ; but he eventually let the sexton of St. Michael's, Wood Street, lay it in the charnel-house."

Towards the end of the reign of Queen Elizabeth the Glaziers' Company do not appear to have been exceptionally prosperous, if we may judge from their contributions to an appeal made by the City Council for some purpose not stated about the year 1590. While the Merchant Tailors were credited with £103 0s. 9d., the contributions of some of the lesser Companies were as follows :—

Glaziers	..	.. 17 7	Minstrels	..	
Basket Makers	..	17 7	Woolmen	.. } each 8 9	
Bowyers	..	.. 11 8	Fletchers..	..	

Again, in 1603, on February 17th, money was collected by the Corporation for railing the streets of London on the occasion of the Queen passing through the City, and a circular was sent out to each Company. Among the responses to the application we find the folllowing :—

Merchant Tailors	37 8 9	Painter Stainers	..	0 8 9
Mercers	.. .. 32 16 0	Armourers ..	..	0 8 0
Clothworkers	.. 22 12 0	Glaziers	.. ..	0 6 4
Dyers	.. .. 4 0 0	Bowyers	.. ..	0 4 0
	Fletchers	.. 0 4 0		

During the Middle Ages the Glaziers and Painters of Glass had been satisfied to remain under the jurisdiction of the City Council as one of the

London Guilds or Fraternities, trusting to the power of that body to redress evils and to grant reasonable rights and privileges. The jurisdiction of the Council did not, however, remain unquestioned during the ages ; occasionally Guilds asserted their entire independence, and it then became necessary for the City to substantiate its overlordship by legal proceedings. When, however, the Council proved its inability to fight successfully against the monopoly of the Crown, the Fraternity of Glaziers had necessarily to invoke the aid of the State Council and ask for a Charter of Incorporation.

CHAPTER IV.

ORIGIN AND RISE OF THE WORSHIPFUL COMPANY OF GLAZIERS
AND PAINTERS OF GLASS—*(continued)*.

IMMEDIATELY upon the death of Queen Elizabeth a coalition of capitalists endeavoured to corner the whole of the business in glass and to adjust prices to suit their own profit; the chiefs were a man named Isaac Bungard* and a certain John Dynes, to which Syndicate one Bringer was subsequently added. Under the régime of these worthies the Guild had perforce to make the best of the circumstances for ten years. It was, however, a strenuous life for them, as may be inferred from the many petitions they addressed to the City Council. The following notices of these have been preserved among the archives.

1609, June 8. It was ordered in Court that a Committee examine and report upon the petition of the Glaziers, but the nature of this petition does not appear. The following petition is the only mention as yet found respecting the transfer of any of the Glaziers to another Company :—

1615. March 1st. Resolved that the Glaziers' Petition that the only Freemen of their Company shall be transferred to the Pewterers' Company be granted.

The Glaziers appear to have sent in another petition the same year since, under notice of a meeting of the Common Council we find :—

1615. On March 20th a Committee was formed at the Lord Mayor's Court to examine into the Petition of the Glaziers', Fruiterers', and Shipwrights' Companies and to consider what should be done to redress their several complaints.

---

* A contract for the supply of glass to Thomas Laurener, Citizen and Goldsmith of London, by Magdalen Bongard, Fernando Bongard and Isaac Bongard, is preserved among the archives of the Glaziers' Company. It is dated Sept. 30, 1595, and is written upon parchment about 23 by 14 inches in size, and is in good preservation. The name of Edward Dobbie, a Glazier, appears upon it, which perhaps explains its preservation in the Company's records.

An Act of Common Council, 1615 (12 James I), ordered Glaziers to be subject to the Masters of the Craft, and very stringent orders, bye-laws, and regulations relating to the general status of apprentices were formulated. This Act may be cited as a corollary naturally following as a sequence to the regulations imposed by the Company's own laws respecting apprentices, and by this means made specially binding by the action of the Common Council.

1616. Sir John Jolles, Kt., Maior. *Item.* A Committee was appointed by the City Council consisting of Sir Thomas Bennett, Sir John Twynton, some of the Aldermen, and others to consider the complaints made by the several Companies of Glaziers, Fruiterers, and Shipwrights and to report thereon.

1616. Oct. 21. Report of the Committee appointed to enquire into the Complaints of the Glaziers.

They report that the Glaziers have been an ancient Brotherhood of the City, and much decayed lately by reason that divers persons of other Companies do pursue their trade and take as many apprentices as they please, whereas if they were Free of the Glaziers they could not have more than one apprentice until they have been Renter Warden and then only two. These persons make what work they please, not being subject to the Search, and discontent has arisen from bad workmanship.

Recommended that all Freemen of other Companies using the trade of a Glazier shall submit to the Search, and that Apprentices taken by them shall be presented to the Master and Wardens of the Glaziers' Company.

This suggestion was allowed, and there follows an Order in Council of very great length concerning the Ancient Brotherhood of Glaziers and embodying the foregoing recommendations.

In connection with this Order in Council it is of interest to note the following, which is found two years later:—

1618, June 6. At this Court the Petition preferred " by such Artizan Glaziers, Freemen of this City as use the arts of Glaziers and are not Free of the Glasyers Company touching the Repeale of an Acte of Council and made 21 October 1616 and in the mairality of Sir John Jolles was here read and considered. The Acte was ordered to remain in force and unrepealed."

The " Right of Search " was undoubtedly one of the most precious and valued prerogatives handed down to the Glaziers, and, so far as is known to the author, this Right has never been lost, repealed, or abrogated, but simply allowed to fall into desuetude. It is possible that in the renaissance of the Glaziers' Company now in active operation the claims may be resuscitated in order to enlarge and widen in some way the sphere of influence for good and useful works now covered by the ancient Guild.

1618. An Act respecting the Glaziers' Company confirming a former Act made 21 Oct., 1616, mentions among other things that the " Carres, Cartes, and Drayes " which the Glaziers of London use were not to be more in number than 400 " Cartes."

In 1610, a Patent was granted to Sir W. Slingsby for making glass by burning coal in furnaces. This innovation in the manner of manufacturing glass was destined to have far-reaching results, for not only did it entirely revolutionise the method of producing the article, but led directly to the production of different varieties of glass by the intense heat produced by coal fires compared with wood, whereby refractory fluxes were fused which had hitherto resisted all efforts. This Patent was revoked in 1615, when James I granted patent rights to Sir Richard Mansell, connected with the Admiralty, to manufacture glass by a method he had devised, using coal for the purpose. The grant is in the names of Mansel, Zouch, Thelwall, Kellaway, and Percivall. At the same time a Royal Proclamation appeared, dated May 23rd, 1615, prohibiting the importation of all foreign glass, while the manufacture of home-produced glass by the use of wood was forbidden, so that Mansell had every possible advantage afforded him at the outset. To do him justice he appears to have conscientiously striven for the good of the glass manufacture, and provided glass by his patent which satisfied the Glaziers and Painters of Glass Guild, as is apparent from a State Paper of April 4th, 1621, reign of James I, which says :—

" The Glaziers' Company of London to the Council. Certify that Sir Robert Mansell's glass is cheap, of good quality, and plentiful, and that it is superior to the glass brought out of Scotland. Are better served now than before when Bungard and others used to buy up all the glass and sell it at high prices."

At the same time there was opposition to Mansell's glass on the part of many Glaziers who apparently were not Free of the Company, and were probably instigated by Bungard. We find the following in the Domestic State Papers :—

March, 1620. Petition of Many Glaziers to the King.

That the proposed Glassworks in Scotland may proceed in order that they may not be compelled to buy Sir R. Mansell's glass which is scarce, bad, and brittle, while of that made in London the best is taken by the undertakers who are Glaziers and yet the rest is sold at full prices.

In the same year (1620) Sir R. Mansell addressed the Council on the several petitions showing that the scarcity of glass was not through any fault of his ; that he had incurred great expense to improve its quality ; and that high prices were due to the rise in the price of coals, but that these prices are lower than before his patent.

In the second Charter of King Charles I to the City of London the duty upon glass entering the port (scavage) is given as—

"Glass for Windows, the chest or case   ..   3*d.*"

March 29, 1620. Meanwhile independent evidence is furnished by the following (also in the State Papers) Certificate by Inigo Jones and Thomas Baldwyn, officers of the Works, that "Sir R. Mansell's glass is mixed good and bad together and is very thin in the middle."

The certificate of competency furnished by the Glaziers' Company as above was not, however, to the taste of the Bungard Coalition, who approached Parliament with a view to upsetting Sir Robert's patent rights, and, knowing by painful experience upon which side their bread was really buttered, the Glaziers petitioned the Royal Commissioners appointed to deal with the business, as follows :—

"1621, April 15. Petition of the Glaziers' Company to the Duke of Lennox and others, Commissioners for the Glass Business. Detail the proceedings of Isaac Bungard, John Dyne and others since 1605 in endeavouring to engross the whole trade in glass so as to have the prices at their disposal ; entreat that their present slanderous bill in

Parliament against Sir Robert Mansell's Patent may be frustrated as the Company must then fall back under their tyranny ; or be subject to the Scottish Patent."

This Petition apparently had weight with the Commissioners and with Parliament, for the application of the capitalists fell through. The Order in Council which resulted is interesting chiefly by reason of the reference it contains to the Royal Prerogative, a subject upon which the young King, Charles I, was even then, after reigning only one year, insistent, and to which by his rigid adherence he eventually lost his head.

1625, Aug. 31. Lady Mansell wrote to the King complaining of the attempt in her husband's absence to overthrow the Patent held by him for manufacturing glass, and urged reasons why the Patent should be continued.

1626. Dec 6. Whitehall—Order of the Council.

The King (Charles I) having referred to those the complaints of one Bringer against the Glass Patent granted to Sir Robert Mansell, it is ordered that the same shall stand. Their lordships think it to be of dangerous consequence and far trenching upon the Prerogative, that Patents granted upon just grounds and of long continuance should be referred to the strict trial of the common law; wherefore, they order that all proceedings at law should be stayed and that Bringer do not presume further to trouble his Majesty on pain of punishment."

It is the unpleasant duty of historians to record those events which do not redound to the credit of the subject of their history as well as those which add to its prestige. It could hardly be expected that the Glaziers' Guild would lead an immaculate existence during the many centuries through which we have followed them, and when we announce that at one time the Master and Wardens were committed to gaol *en bloc*, we do not feel that shock of complete surprise and pain which perhaps we should. The account of the discreditory transaction is as follows :—

In December, 1627, an Act of Common Council was passed agreeing to furnish the King (Charles I) with a loan of £120,000, of which £60,000 was to be handed over within ten days. Precepts were accordingly issued to the

City Companies to provide their proportion of the amount. Because the Masters and Wardens of the Glaziers', the Saddlers', and the Fruiterers' Companies did not use their best endeavours to carry out the precept of the Lord Mayor, the said dignitaries were incarcerated in Newgate Prison. This high-handed proceeding necessitated the Royal Assent and the following Order in Council was issued :—

" *Whitehall, 10th February, 1627.*

" In refusing to submit to the Order in Council enjoyning them to paye their severale partes towards the raising of the sum which the Citye had contracted to supply the King for the defence of the Realm. His Majesty approved of the proceedyngs of the Courte of Aldermen and ratified them their decysion by an Order in Council signifying that the said persons should not be enlarged until his further pleasure was known and ordered that the commitments be ratified and continued."

As these demands for money were generally made with no ulterior desire of repayment, and the three Companies mentioned were undoubtedly cognisant of the fact, our strictures, if any, upon their conduct will, we feel sure, be extremely mild.

1633, Nov. 19. Thursday next is by this Court appointed for hearing of the Cause of Complaynte made by the Companie of Glasirs against one Thomas Bayley free of the Girdlers but useing the trade of a glasier.

On October 14th, 1634, Complaint was made to the London Council against John Bargeman for taking two apprentices when he was only entitled to one, but by the " Science and Misterie of Glazing Company " or, in other words, " The Glaziers' Company," Bargeman was ordered to conform himself as a loving brother to the Glaziers' Company and to put away his second apprentice."

The Mansell glass continued in use with apparently satisfactory results for a time, but eight years after the Bungard action had been quashed, complaints were made by the Glaziers concerning the deterioration of the glass, which eventually led up to the statement before the Privy Council by Sir Robert, in which he tabulated the reasons for the production of the inferior quality, as follows :—

1634, Jan. 28. Reign of Charles I.

" Statement of the costs, difficulties and losses of Sir Robert Mansell in
the business of glass. He was out of purse above £30,000 before the
manufacture could be perfected, notwithstanding which, in his
absence at Algiers, his Patent was declared void by the House of
Commons. The consideration of his charges moved the late King
(James I) to grant him a Patent for 15 years, but, before he could
obtain any fruit of that Patent, his workmen and servants were
drawn into Scotland, and most of the glass here was importation
from thence, whereupon he was obliged to purchase the Scottish
Patent for £250 per annum. After his men returned from Scotland
they made such ill-conditioned glass that he was forced to procure
a whole company from Mantua. For window glass the price is now
certain and more moderate than formerly. Albeit the assize is more
now by 40 feet than it used to be. His men are again drawn into
Scotland, glass is attempted to be made in Ireland and Crispe, his
tenant, endeavours to obtain a branch of the Patent and offers for
the whole."

This statement appears to have had the effect intended, for, after a decent
delay of a year and a-half, a Royal Proclamation dated October 14th, 1635,
appeared prohibiting the importation of all kinds of glass made in foreign parts.
It recites the proclamation of James I, dated May 23rd, 1625, prohibiting the
use of wood in making of glass and also the importation of foreign glass. It
asserts also that Sir Robert Mansell, Lieutenant of the Admiralty, had perfected the manufacture of glass with sea coal or pit coal to the saving of the
wood of the Kingdom, nevertheless divers ill-affected persons presume to
import foreign glass.

The cost of leaded glass at that time is of interest and may be appro-
priately entered here. A bill is given in the State Papers, dated June 4th,
1636, being the account of Richard Butler for £62 7s. 6d. for glazing the north
and west windows of Archbishop Laud's Chapel at Lambeth House. The
charge for new-leading old glass was 18d. the foot ; that for new glass and
fixing was 6s. the foot.

For two years after the proclamation of 1635 the " Glaziers and Painters of Glass " Fraternity used the bad material supplied to them without any manifest signs of their discontent, but, meanwhile, were preparing for the coup which would enlist the State upon their side in any action they might meditate against those who supplied inferior glass.   On May 5th, 1637, the Petition was in the hands of the State Council and in the wording of it one admires the method of procedure, whereby the real object of their petition is not specifically named, but they ask for protection against those who transgress in other ways.

> 1637, May 5.   " Petition of the Fraternity of the Glaziers of London to the King.   Divers persons useing the trade of Glaziers and Painters of Glass in London used many deceits in the draught of their lead beyond the proportioned length of the weight thereof ; in keeping rules of a prohibited length ; in working false and deceitful materials ; and in handling the same falsely.   They pray for an Incorporation of the present Freemen of that trade within London and five miles compass."
>
> (a) This paper was referred to the Attorney-General to certify his opinion, St. James, May 5th, 1637.
>
> (b) Report of Attorney-General Bankes :—" I do not discern any inconvenience if your Majesty please to incorporate the Petitioners."
>
> (c) Further referred to the Attorney-General to prepare the Grant of Incorporation, Whitehall, June 5th, 1637.

The Charter of Incorporation is dated November 6th, 1638.   It should be noted that the two Heraldic Visitations referred to in Cap. V occurred previously to the above date and serve to prove, if such were necessary, that the Glaziers and Painters of Glass held an accredited and honourable position among the Guilds of London during the mediaeval times, which was possibly by no means added to, or accentuated in any particular, upon their incorporation.

A perusal of the history of the Company during the first part of the seventeenth century will undoubtedly lead the reader to infer that the names of

Isaac Bungard and John Dynes were obnoxious to the Company of Glaziers, inasmuch as they stood for extortion, oppression, and the triumph of capital over labour. Even the judges had to administer a severe rebuke to the syndicate of which they were the leaders (*vide* p. 31). The measure of our surprise is therefore considerable when we find the names of these worthies among the honoured list of those who sought for and obtained the Charter of Incorporation of King Charles I. They occur as numbers six and seven respectively in a list of twenty-four names, thus showing conclusively that they were not recent additions to the livery. The name of Isaac Bungard appears in Lease No. 13 (*vide* p. 44) as one of the grantees to property in Fyve Foot Lane; in other words, of property forming part of, or adjacent to, the Glaziers' Hall. This was in 1624. It would almost appear that the two repented of their misdeeds and showed their sincerity by seeking admission into the Fraternity of which they had been the mortal enemies; or else, finding that opposition to the Glaziers brought them nothing but odium, they thought it more advisable to coalesce than to remain at variance. Or peradventure the advances were first made by the Company, who thought that the alliance might strengthen their application for a Charter? As no documentary evidence, so far as we know, is extant upon the point the Glaziers of the present day are free to indulge in any pleasing conjectures they may choose.

With the granting of the Charter of Incorporation the Glaziers and Painters of Glass Company proceeded to carry out their primary object, *i.e.*, the impeachment of Sir Robert Mansell and his coadjutors, but before this occurrence, a brother Company, the Glass Sellers, whose functions are specifically stated in their Charter (1664) as " makers and sellers of looking glasses, and sellers (not makers) of glasses, bottles, pots, etc.," entered a remonstrance against Sir Robert alleging that his glass was so bad that much of it was unusable and had to be thrown away. Whether they did this to help the indictment by the Glaziers is not known, but as it was made on December 15th, 1637, it no doubt strengthened the petition of the latter, which was lodged with the Council of State on January 12th, 1638.

Whitehall. " Order of Council upon the complaint of the Company of Glaziers against Sir Robert Mansell and his contractors in reference to the dearness, badness, and scarcity of glass and the want of full size. Sir

R. Mansell answered that the dearness was the result of the rise in price of all the materials ; that the scarcity was occasioned by the mortality that fell among the workmen at Newcastle during the late visitation (*i.e.*, of the plague) and since for want of shipping, and that, as to the badness, he agreed that whatever proved nought at the making should be broken at the furnace. These answers seemed reasonable, but the Lords, having found by their own experience that the glass was not so fair, so clear, nor so strong as the same was wont to be, ordered that Sir Robert should take effectual care in these particulars."

It was further objected that Sir Robert had contracted for all his glass with Lancelot Hobson, so that the Glaziers could have none but such as he thought fit, and that he cut the glass into quarries, and made a reservation at Newcastle of the best glass. It was thought fit that the contract with Hobson should be dissolved, and that the cutters should be withdrawn from Newcastle, and no more be cut there, with a variety of other regulations to ensure the Glaziers a proper supply and at a reasonable price.

1640, Sep. 15. Sir Robt. Mansell to the Sec., Windebank, made a statement concerning his glass works at Newcastle. He had spent £4,000 on the furnaces and employed 60 workmen. Asks for two, three, or four ships to fetch away his glass and to bring coal.

The reference to Newcastle in the foregoing is of interest because Sir Robert in 1623 had stated that the furnaces erected in London, the Isle of Purbeck, Milford Haven, and on the Trent had all failed, but that they had been successful at Newcastle-on-Tyne ; it appears to infer that the initial success at Newcastle had been maintained.

1639. The "Saltpetremen" petitioned the Crown against Sir R. Mansell, and in self-justification Mansell replied : " I have done nothing for the furnishing of His Majesty's glass works with ashes but what shall be warranted by the broad seal of England and the contentment of the whole country."

CHAPTER V.

WHEN the writing of this History was commenced a tradition was prevalent in the Company that a Glaziers' Hall once existed and that it perished in the Great Fire of London, 1666. The investigation into this matter has involved considerable time and research, chiefly owing to the fact that no available data was forthcoming from the archives of the Company, due in the main to the catastrophe of 1870, whereby the majority of the parchment deeds were irretrievably destroyed (*vide* extracts from Minutes, 1870). It is true that compensation for the damage, to the amount of £30, was subsequently received by the Company, but that sum, in the light of the valuable records injured, appears to be far from adequate. The writing upon the parchments in some cases has been almost entirely removed, in others blank patches occur with illegible writing surrounding them. By the natural Law of Fatality the undecipherable portions occur in the most valuable evidential parts of the parchments.

The first clue to the locale of "Glaziers' Hall" was given by an almost illegible endorsement upon the back of No. 16 Deed, which, in 19th century writing, reads:—"late Glaziers' Hall, in Parish of St. Bennett, Ward of Castle Baynard." The next reward after a diligent search was the reading of "——— commonly called Glaziers' Hall" in a marginal curl of No. 8, an indenture of 1612. These documents make mention of an indenture, with a schedule attached, between the Company of Fishmongers and a William Blewd. It fortunately happens that one parchment, No. 6, of 15th February, 1601, is the least damaged by water and can be almost fully deciphered. It relates to the lease of a tenement sometime part of Old

Fishmongers' Hall to a William Blewd, and has a schedule appended, hence the clue is a complete one.

It would appear that the Fishmongers' Company possessed a Hall in Five Foot Lane (now Fye Foot Lane), lying between Old Fish Street (Queen Victoria Street) and Thames Street, with a frontage to Old Fish Street Hill, and, as that Company still possesses property upon the eastern side of Fye Foot Lane, the Hall presumably stood there. The Fishmongers leased the Hall and gave the tenant the power to sub-lease it. The Glaziers' Company appears to have taken it over, and also subsequently to have acquired building leases near, since new buildings pertaining to the Company of Glaziers are mentioned in Deed No. 13, and an indenture of March 15th, 1624, as standing in Five Foot Lane in the parish of St. Mary. The Hall and its adjacent property would seem to have been in different parishes and Wards, hence confusing references occur to "St. Mary Mounthawe, Ward of Castle Baynard," "Queen Hythe Ward," "parish of St. Bennett," "the church house in the parish of ——— in the Winter" (*i.e.*, Vintry)—all of which appear to indicate the same site. The whole of this property was swept away in the Great Fire of 1666, but, presumably, the Clerk had charge of the documents relating to the Company, and this accounts for their preservation. It is within the bounds of possibility that the Company may at some future period acquire some of the Fye Foot Lane property and erect a Hall upon or near the site where their ancient Guild used to meet.

The schedule referred to above as being annexed to Lease No. 6, dated 13th February, 1601, has been transcribed and inserted here. It is probably the only description extant of Old Glaziers' Hall, and as such is of great interest :—

SCHEDULE OF LEASE DATED 13TH FEBRUARY, 1601.

" This Shedule Indented

"Conteyneth and Mencoeth [mentioneth] the Wainskotte and complem^{ts} demised by the Indenture of Lease hereunto annexed and are remayning to and in the messuage or tenem^{ts} Demised by the same Indenture *Viz.*

" In the Hall of the same Messuage.

" The Hall is Boorded about with bords which are painted like Wainskott And the same Hall is setled [furnished with settles or seats] on the South side and the next side with two bords.

" In the plor [parlour] *adioyning to the Hall.*

" The chymney there is trymmed to the wainskott and at the one end of the same chymney there is a Court Cubbord wrought and fastened with the wainskott and at thother end of the chymney two Cubbords wainskott The same plor is settled with wainsskott before the Doore of wainskott going into the Kithcen And all the same plor is saving a little peece thereof betweene the Dore Coming out of the Hall and the window is wainscotted.

" In the Kitchen

" There are three thicke plancks set upp for Kitchen Bords one long and two short.

" In the Chamber over the Plor.

" The same Chamber is hanged round about in the painted Clothe being white hunted worke.

" In the Courte Yeard.

" The Frame Wood over the Well and the handel of Iron to drawe water withall."

Unfortunately the Fishmongers' Company does not possess any plan of their property in Five Foot Lane, Old Fish Street Hill, or Thames Street, as it existed before the Great Fire, and therefore cannot definitely locate the site occupied by Old Fishmongers' Hall, while the plans of their estate, executed since 1666, afford little or no clue to the ichnography of the district before that date. Stowe says : " that upon the Eastern side of Old Fish Street Hill stood a great House belonging to the Fishmongers which was afterwards let out to rent as, before the Fire, they had six Hall Motes, viz.: two in Bridge Street or New Fish Street, two in Old Fish Street whereof this was one, and two in Stockfishmonger Row or Thames Street." The authority for this statement is a document, *temp*. Richard II. Maitland alludes to Fish Street Hill as a " well-inhabited place." He also speaks of "a fair House in the Parish of St. Mary Mounthaw now letten out for Rent, which house some time was one of the Halls pertaining to the Company of Fishmongers," and incidentally mentions that "on the north side of St. Nicholas Cole Abbey Church in the wall thereof was built a convenient Cistern of Stone and Lead for receipt of Thames Water conveyed in Pipes of Lead to that place for the use and commodity of the

MAP OF LONDON, BY AGAS (*temp.* Q. Eliz., *c.* 1560), preserved in the Guildhall.

(Glaziers' Hall, to 1666, had a frontage to Fysche Streate Hill, and extended upon the East side of Fyve Foot Lane (marked with a *).   It was either the building shown at the North-West corner abutting upon Old Fysche Streate or the one immediately below in Fysche Streate Hill.   The entrance to Fyve Foot Lane from Tames Streate, or Stockfishmonger Row, was apparently through an archway.)

Fishmongers and the other inhabitants in and about Old Fish Street.   This was completed about 1583."   With regard to the new property erected by the Glaziers, the Fishmongers' Company have documentary evidence that the Glaziers sought a lease of land adjacent to the Hall and offered to erect property upon it to the value of £200, but the City Authorities were not willing to agree to the lease, deeming the money inadequate.   It is obvious that the sum offered must have been increased, inasmuch as the property was built.

St. Mary Mounthaw Church was not rebuilt after the Fire.   The Parish was added to St. Mary Somerset (the church whose isolated tower still stands in Thames Street though the nave has disappeared) while the site was converted into a burying place. It is described by Stowe as being small and originally a Chapel of the Mounthaut family; it had been enlarged in 1609 and was wholly glazed in 1610. Regarding the nomenclature of Fye Foot Lane, it appears to have been originally Finnemore Lane, altered to Five Foot Lane because it narrowed to that width at its

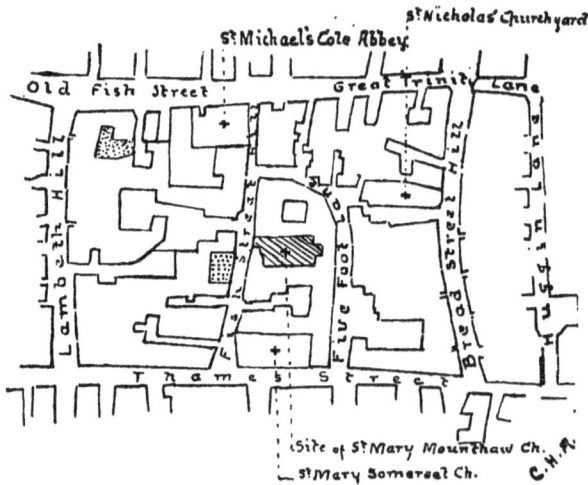

MAP OF LONDON, BY MAITLAND, 1760.

(Fish Street Hill, or Labour in Vain Hill (now built over), had Five Foot Lane running into it.   Five Foot Lane, or Finnimore Lane (the present Fye Foot Lane), had a narrow lane, called Star Lane, running from it to Old Fish Street (now Queen Victoria Street).   The two lanes have been straightened and named Fye Foot Lane.)

western end.   This western end joined Old Fish Street Hill, which, owing to the march of improvement in erecting buildings in this locality, has entirely disappeared.

A LIST OF ANCIENT DEEDS, ETC., IN POSSESSION
OF THE COMPANY.

(For the greater part indecipherable by reason of an overflow of water into
the cellar of Radley's Hotel in 1570.)

No.	Date.	Reign.	
1.	1546, Oct. 27.	Hy. VIII.	—Petition of the Foreign Glaziers to the Star Chamber. The greater part is illegible, but "foren glazyers of the said [Citie]," "treating of dyvers . . . ." and odd words are decipherable.
2.	1546.	Hy. VIII.	—Apparently some rules of the Fishmongers' Company. " Ye Wardens beying set in ye . . ." " at ye Knocke of a hamer," and a few other phrases may be read.
3.	1577, Sep. 20.	Q. Eliz.	—Deed Poll by the Company of Glaziers. It recites an indenture of Sept. 24, 1576. The name of Richard Cartwright may be made out, but the deed is almost illegible.
*4.	1578, July 14.	Q. Eliz.	—A lease for 21 years. Myles Mason and Edward , Citizens and Glaziers of London, to John Smythe. "Over the said cellar and roome," " Wardens and Assistants" can be read. It relates to a tenement called " The Churche Howse" in the Parish of —— in the Winter [? Vintry]. On the back, in 19th century writing, may be read " Church House, St. Martin's Vestry."
*5.	1595. — —	Q. Eliz.	—Indenture between Madalen Bongard, of Greenwich, Widow, and Isaac Bongard, of

* Where the numbers of the documents are thus distinguished (*), it signifies that the parchment in question is worthy of renovation and being put into a condition which would ensure its preservation. Remembering that the present generation is the custodian of the historical records of the next, it is undoubtedly the duty of those living to endeavour to preserve the records of the past handed down to them as intact as possible to those who are to follow.

Greenwich, gent., of the one part, and
Thomas Lawrence, citizen and goldsmith, of
London, of the other part. A Contract
with respect to payment for glass. Five
hundred cases of Normandy glass are mentioned.

*6. 1601, Feb. 15. Q. Eliz.—The Wardens and Commonalty of the
Mistery of Fishmongers to William Blewe,
Citizen and Fishmonger.

In consideration of £50, lease of their Great
Messuage or Tenement wherein Robert
Hopton, late of London, esquire, did dwell
and was sometime part of a great tenement
called Old Fishmongers' Hall, in sort, as the
same Messuage or Tenement is divided and
secured from other Tenements of the same
Old Hall and four cellars under part of the
same, late in the tenure of Roger Hole,
Fishmonger.

[The short Schedule appended to this lease,
describing the Hall and its contents, appears
in the former part of this Chapter.]

7. 1610, Oct. 8. James I—Indenture by which Sara Blewe of London,
Widow, consigns to Reginald Hughes a
lease by the Fishmongers' Company dated
15 Feb., 1601, of their great tenement parcel
of the Old Fishmongers' Hall.

[An endorsement on the back, in contemporary writing, reads: "The consignment from
Mrs. Blewe to Mr. Hughes of the new hall,"
but the meaning of "new" is proble-
matical.]

No.	Date.	Reign.

*8.   1612, Feb. 27.   James I.—Indenture made between John Rowse, etc., of the Glaziers' Company of the one part and Thomas Arem of the other part. The said John Rowse and others of the Company lease to the said Thomas Arem for seven years a messuage or Tenement in . . . . [The name of the property is illegible.]

*9.   1612, Dec. 2.   James I.—Indenture between Reginald Hughes, citizen and Fishmonger of London, and John Rowse, Master of the Glaziers' Company, the Wardens, etc. Refers to lease of 15 Feb., 1601, and states that the lease has been conveyed to Reginald Hughes by Sara Blewe on 8 Oct., 1610. The said Reginald Hughes assigns to the said John Rowse, etc., the said rented lease.

10.   1613, Dec. 2.   James I.—This document is an Act of Common Council and appears to have reference to Apprentices. The common seal of the City of London is appended to it. It is torn, much defaced, and in very bad condition.

*11.   1619, Apr. 14.   James I.—A Warrant of Search. Empowers the Master and Wardens of the Company of Glaziers to make the Search when deemed necessary.

*12.   1620, May 5.   James I.—Indenture between John Rouse, Christopher Collett, etc. . . . . . Company of Glaziers of the City of London. Lease for 2¾ years of Tenements adjoining Old Fishmongers' Hall in the Parish of St. Mary Mounthawe.

*13.   1624, Mar. 2.   James I.—Indenture between Christopher Collard, Isaac Bunger, and others, Glaziers, of the

No.	Date.	Reign.

one part, and Rinell Herbert, citizen and Embroiderer of London, of the other part. Lease of one chamber, one room . . . . two chambers . . . . in Fyve Foot Lane in the parish of St. Mary Mounthawe in the Ward of Queenhithe. With a covenant that the Company of Fishmongers may enter to search. Rent £10 . 10 . 0.

*14. 1624, Mar. 15. James I.—An Indenture between Christopher Collard of . . . . and others and Anthony Newlove. Lease of a cellar, a room, or hall, above the same cellar . . . . and rooms next the new buildings appertaining to the Company of Glaziers in Fyve Foot Lane in the Parish St. Mary. With a covenant that the Company of Fishmongers may enter and twice a year search the said tenements. Rent £10 . . . . shillings.

15. 1644, Mar. 25. Chas. I. —Indenture between Charles Rowse, Citizen and Glazier of London, of the one part, and Richard Campion, Master of the Company Glaziers in the City of London, of the other part, dated 25 ———, 1644 : Recites that the Master and Commonalty of the Mistery of Fishmongers, by lease (8 June, 1615) demised to Robert Hopton, Esq., a messuage or tenement , . . . called Old Fishmongers' Hall, for 32 years. The said John Rowse assigns the said recited Lease and the said tenements, vault or cellar, room or garret, to the said Richard Campion.

16. 1720, Sep. 29. George I.—Loriners' Company to Glaziers' Company, Lease of rooms, etc. [illegible], adjoining

No.	Date.	Reign.	
			to London Wall and Basinghall Street. Endorsed "Part of Loriners' Hall."
17.	— —	George I.	—Illegible, but evidently an Indenture of Lease. It is possible that parts of it might be read after the application of a solution.
18.	16—Mar. 19	—	—The names of Abraham Chitty, Edmund Milman, Richard Campion, Baptist Sutton, and Edward Brus can be read. The description of the property cannot be deciphered as yet. As the name of Richard Campion appears in Deed No. 15, this deed is probably also early 17th century, while the name of Baptist Sutton appears as an Assistant in the Charter of Charles I. It is at present in a hopeless condition.
19.	— —	—	—A piece of parchment, a few inches square, containing some illegible writing. Probably a Schedule.

CHAPTER VI.

THE ARMS OF THE COMPANY IN 1588.

THE exact date when the Arms of the Company were granted is unknown, but the first description of them occurs in 1588, reign of Queen Elizabeth, when the Herald, Robert Cooke, Clarencieux King of Arms, made his official visit to the Company. These inspections were necessary in mediaeval times, and carried out also during the Renaissance, in order to ensure that no false or spurious heraldry was being used, and were termed "Heraldic Visitations." A second Visitation was made in 1634, and the account is duly recorded in the College of Arms as follows :—

The Armes, Creast and Supporters of the Corporation and Fellowship of the Glaziers of the Cittie of London testified under the hand of Robert Cooke, Clarencieux King of Armes, 1588, in a peice of Vellam and now veiwed and approved in the Visitation of London, made by Sr. Hen: St. George Kt. Richmond 1634. At which tyme John Addison was Master and William Hide and Eusebius Pallmos wardens.

Edmond Roberts Clark to the said Companye.

The Arms granted to the Company, and duly recorded in the College of Arms, are of considerable interest from several points of view. They are as follows (*vide* beginning of book) :—

Shield.—Argent, two glazing irons in saltire sable between four closing nails of the last, on a chief gules a lion passant guardant or.

Crest.—On a wreath of the colours a lion's head couped or, between two wings expanded azure.

Supporters.—Two naked boys proper, each holding in his exterior hand a long torch inflamed of the last.

Motto.—" Lucem tuam da nobis, O Deus."

As the jargon of heraldic terms which crept into the Art of Heraldry during the 14th and 15th centuries has never, unfortunately, been abolished, the following transliteration of the foregoing rendered into English may be acceptable.

Shield.—On a silver ground two black glazing irons (" Grazing irons " in some descriptions, from Fr. *gresoir*, a flat notched strip of iron used for breaking off small chips from the edges of cut glass), placed like a saltire, the name given to the St. Andrew's Cross, which is shaped like a capital X. They lie between four black closing nails.   Upon the upper third of the shield, called the chief, and depicted red, is a lion passant, or walking, and guardant, *i.e.*, with the face turned towards the spectator.   He is represented in gold. It is stated that in the earliest arms this lion was represented as a demi-lion, and that Sir Richard St. George altered it to a lion passant.

Crest.—The wreath is coloured red and blue, and is really the orle or ring of twisted material which is supposed by some to have been worn by Knights round the bascinet to distribute the weight of the great heaume, or helm, when worn over it, or else to be the mantling wrapped round the bascinet.   Upon the wreath is a lion's head in gold couped or cut off evenly, lying between two blue expanded wings.

Supporters.—Two naked boys represented in their proper colour, not heraldic, hold in their right and left hands respectively a lighted torch, also in natural colours.

Motto.—" Lucem tuam da nobis, O Deus," which may be rendered " Give us thy light, O God," or more freely, " Illuminate us with thy light, O God," which, by bearing a readily-discernible secondary meaning in the invocation to the Almighty, would be acceptable to all.   This motto has varied at times and appeared as " Da nobis lucem, Domine," " Give us light, O Lord " ; " Lumen umbra Dei," " Light and darkness are of God," or " Light is the shadow of God " (?). " Non sine lumine," " Nothing is possible without light," and " Fiat Lux," " Let there be light."

The supporters are interesting because the human figure, although it often appears " *in nudas veritas* " upon the shield is almost unique in this particular use as supporters ; probably the only other example extant are the supporters in the arms of the Joiners' Livery Company, where two naked boys occur, one holding an emblematical female figure and the other a square. " Savages " are, of course, often depicted, but are invariably represented in laurel wreaths.

In modern times the partial clothing of the two boys has been introduced and the scarves used in this connection have been rendered blue ; there is no justification whatever for this innovation, as the terms of the grant are explicit and definite. The arms as at present delineated partake too much of Queen Anne flamboyance of a debased character to be either pleasing or satisfactory to one cognisant of the ancient origin of the Company, and a new design by a competent artist, versed in mediaeval heraldry, with helmet, mantling, heater-shield, etc., would form not only a graceful gift to the Guild, but also be of the greatest use.

The Gateshead Glazing Company bear the same arms as the " Glaziers and Painters of Glass " of London, with the exception of the motto ; they were granted in 1671.

CHAPTER VII.

THE REGALIA.

THE *Table Cloth* of 1646. This Table Cloth is of considerable length, of woollen material, and bears in the centre the initials "D.B." worked in wool embroidery and the date 1646. The initials are about six inches in height and the numerals less than two inches. There is no clue forthcoming as yet respecting the donor, if the two letters are his initials, but one cannot help regarding the juxtaposition of these two letters as extremely significant since they are the initial letters of "Dynes" and "Bungard," the erstwhile mortal enemies of the Glaziers. Unfortunately there is no Minute Book of that date, but if, seven years after the Incorporation, John Dynes and Isaac Bungard became respectively Master and Upper Warden of the Company, the mystery would be explained. This is a purely hypothetical surmise on the part of the Author, and as such is suggested with all due deference.

The Streamers. These are four in number, and are all based upon the same model, namely, that of the mediaeval standard. They measure 13½ feet in length, and are three feet wide in the broadest part ; the material is silk. They have bifurcated terminations and are painted upon both sides, and have the edges fringed. Upon the widest portion of the banner, and occupying approximately one quarter of the total length, the arms of the City of London appear, next to which those of the Glaziers occur. The third portion of the banner is occupied with the Glaziers' crest, and the fourth or last part is filled with a conventional design in the style of the Renaissance. The whole achievement is emblazoned in the Livery colours as detailed in the grant of arms of 1588. Three of the streamers are in a worn and faded condition and are probably those made in 1706, but the fourth is evidently more recent (probably 1753, *vide p.* 82), and shows but little sign of use.

The *Table Cloth* of June 4th, 1706, and the Streamers. "And it is by this Court ordered declared and agreed that the Master and Wardens, Mr. Philip Narraway, Mr. Henry Anger, Mr. Thomas Sarny, Mr. James Thompson, Mr. William Price, Mr. Henry Bray and Mr. William Purgour or any three or more of them with the Master and Wardens shall be a Committee and are hereby authorized and impowered forthwith to provide buy and pay for at the costs and charges of this Company and for their use and service three new silk Flags or Streamers with their appurtenances answerable and agreeable to those flags or streamers now belonging unto this Company And likewise that they the said Committee shall at the like costs and charges and for the like use and service provide buy and pay for One new large Cloth whereon shall be imbroidered the Arms of Her Majesty Queen Ann, this City and this Company. And to that end and purpose they the said Committee shall forthwith agree with and imploy fitt and skilfull workmen for the doing and performing and finding and providing the severall works and workmanships and materialls needfull for the making and furnishing the said new streamers and cloth according to the good discretion of this Committee."

The Beadle's Staff.—The head of the staff is of silver, weighing 1½ lbs., and probably contains twelve or more ounces of the pure metal. The actual date of manufacture, and also of presentation to the Company is unknown as no Hall Mark is discernible, and the inscription round the pedestal simply reads—
        " The gift of Ioh : Oliver a loving member of this Company."
without any date.   The earliest entry of John Oliver's name is to be found in 1698, September 21st, where at a Quarterly Court held on that day at Loriners' Hall he was present.   The names of the Assistants attending are entered in the margin as was usual, with no distinctive mark, but John Oliver has " Esquire " following his name, from which we may infer that his position was somewhat different to the rest.

The head of the staff is fashioned in the form of a boy, nude, holding a staff, now broken off, in the right hand, the upper part probably terminated at one time in a torch, thus representing one of the supporters of the Company's arms.   The left hand rests upon the upper part of a foliated cartouche resting upon the ground, in the centre of which a raised oval shield is repoussé, upon which the Glaziers' Arms are engraved without the motto. The figure, which is six inches in height, stands upon a pedestal encircled by three narrow raised bands consisting of a half-round bead flanked by two fillets. Between the two upper bands the Motto is engraved " Lucem tuam da nobis, o Deus." The pedestal measures four inches in height and is furnished with an iron screw for affixing it to the wooden staff.

The Master's Jewel.—The Master's badge is of silver-gilt, bearing red, blue, and black enamel. In the centre occur the floreated arms of the Company, surmounted by a lion's head coupée regardant winged. The lion is of gold upon red enamel ; the glazing irons and closing nails are in black enamel upon silver. The motto " Lucem tuam da nobis, o Deus," is in gold upon blue enamel. Upon the back is engraved " P. M. Badge of Charles Enos Fenton, Esq., 1886-1887."

The Upper Warden's Jewel. — The Upper Warden's badge is of silver and enamel similar in design to that of the Master. It was the Master's Badge until 1900, but was presented in that year by Mr. Harry Seymour Foster.

The Seal of the Company.—The Seal of the Company is of silver and is probably contemporary in date with the granting of the Charter in 1638. There is no date or Hall Mark upon it, but the initials I.A. occur, and may possibly be those of John Addison, whose name occurs in the list of Assistants to whom the Carolean Charter is granted. There was a Joseph Alwintale in 1781, and a John Armitage in 1823, but the design of the seal appears to preclude the possibility of its being so late in date.

The Spicer Loving Cup is the oldest Cup in possession of the Company. It bears the following inscription :—

" Presented to the Glaziers' Company by Edward Samuel Spicer, a liveryman of the Company, 1901."

The Edmunds Punch Bowl and Ladle. — This massive and imposing piece of Silver is a magnificent example of American workmanship.

The bowl is of imposing dimensions and has modelled bands of alto-relievo work around the bowl and the base.   It rests upon a plinth of light oak.   The ladle is of the lily pattern and has repoussé work of an appropriate character for a loving cup upon the handle.   It bears the following inscription :—

" This Bowl and Ladle being excellent examples of American Craftsman-ship in Silver, manufactured by the Mauser Company was purchased by Henry Edmunds, Master, in New York in January 1912 and presented by him to the Worshipful Company of Glaziers through William James Berriman Tippetts, C.C., the Clerk of the Company, for their use and safe keeping ; also as a token of regard for Past Master George Paget Walford who proposed and introduced the said Henry Edmunds and his dear friend William Paul James Fawcus, since deceased, who became Members of the Company in 1886 and 1905 respectively.   The Donor also wishes to refer to his dear and respected friend Robert Dyas who was his immediate pre-decessor in the Master's Chair and who died in office, during the visit of Henry Edmunds to America and whose sad loss was greatly felt by all the Members of the Worshipful Company, to which he had belonged for 23 years."

This Bowl and Ladle were presented to the Worshipful Company of Glaziers, for their use and safe keeping as long as they shall remain a Company.

From Henry Edmunds, Master, A.D. 1912.

The two Walford Loving Cups.—These massive Cups are of excellent workmanship of the hanap type with covers.   They are mounted upon black plinths and bear the following inscription upon one side :—

" Presented to the Worshipful Company of Glaziers and Painters of Glass by George Paget Walford, as a slight token of his appreciation of the unique honour he has enjoyed in having been elected three times to occupy the Chair as Master of the Company, 1904, 1917, 1918."

Upon the reverse side of the Cups the Arms of the Company are engraved.

The back of the Master's Chair is surmounted by:—

The Arms of the Glaziers' Company, beautifully carved in wood. The whole achievement is enamelled in the appropriate heraldic colours and forms a most effective finial.

The Arms of the Company emblazoned upon glass, presented by Mr. Charles F. Fenton, represent the supporters in blue scarves, and therefore probably date from the middle of the eighteenth century, but might possibly be older. The achievement has been repaired where necessary, and mounted in a frame for preservation.

Photographic Album.—This Album, of large dimensions and bound in morocco leather, is preserved in an oaken case with the Arms of the Company engraved thereon in brass.

It was presented to the Company by Mr. James Berriman Tippetts (Clerk 1887-1898) in 1889. It contains a dedicatory poem by the donor, well meriting insertion in this book:—

When first our pious Ancestors besought
  Th' Eternal Power to give His blessed light,
They little deemed the precious boon they sought
  Would, in the future, by its subtle might
(By Skill directed, and by Science taught),
  Preserve "Our Worthies" to our mortal sight,
E'en when, in fulness of their honoured age,
Their parts well played they quit Earth's troubled stage.
  Within this Volume, by the Mystic power
Of the Great Gift, our Motto humbly asks—
  They live again beyond this transient hour ;
Their works completed, and perform'd their tasks.
    May they enjoy the day that knows no night,
    And in the shadow of their God, find perfect light.

CHAPTER VIII.

THE MASTERS AND WARDENS—(*Pre-Incorporation*).

Year.	Reign.		Master.	Upper Warden.
1328.	Edward III	..	John Husbonde	Alan Gille
1368.	,,		Henry Stannermore	William Papelwyk
1373.	,,	..	John de Brampton	John Geddyngge
1381.	Richard II	..	Richard Sauvage	William Pathe
1384.	,,	..	John Byford	Henry Bourne
1391.	,,	..	Thomas Manfield	Simon Page
1420.	Henry V	..	John Wittelesey	William Eveyot
1425.	Henry VI	..	John Wittelesey	John Greylond
1432.	,,	..	John Greylond	Richard Harman
1438.	,,	..	John Greylond	Robert Whiteker
1518.	Henry VIII	..	Robert Nelson	John Aleyne
1523.	,,	..	John Stone	William Hatton
1525.	,,	..	Henry Pepwell	Lewys Sutton
1528.	,,	..	John Mylford	John Wabe
1562.	Q. Elizabeth	..	— —	— —
				(*Beadle*—J. Paine,)
1612.	James I	..	John Pont	John Butterfield,
	Assistants—Richard Spearman			Christopher Collard
	Lionel Bennett			John Dynes
1634.	Charles I	..	John Addison	Eusebius Pallnor
				(*Clerk*—Edmond Roberts)

THE MASTERS, WARDENS AND CLERKS—*(Post Incorporation)*.

The Masters and Wardens take office on St. Andrew's Day, November 30th, in each year.

Year.	Master.	Upper Warden.	Clerk and Beadle.
1644.	Campion, Richard	Ellis, Thomas	

Six Assistants—Thomas Herbert · · · Edward Hygge · · · Nrm. Hide
Richard Sutton · · · Francis Pates · · · Robert Porwith

Year.	Master.	Upper Warden.	Clerk and Beadle.
1697.	Sarney, Thomas	Price, William	Brandon, Gilbert (*was Clerk in* 1694) (Stacey, Thomas, Beadle)
1698.	Thompson, James	Hill, John	
1699.	Price, William	Bray, Henry	
1700.	Bray, Henry	Watson, Robert	
1701.	Watson, Robert	Puryour, William	
1702.	Puryour, William	Auery, Edward	
1703.	Avery, Edward	Carter, William	
1704.	Carter, William	Charnley, Richard	
1705.	Charnley, Richard	Proudlove, John	
1706.	Proudlove, John	Fletcher, Thomas	
1707.	Fletcher, Thomas	Goodchild, James	
1708.	Goodchild, James	Gurnett, Thomas	
1709.	Narraway, Philip	Cooper, John	
1710.	Cooper, John	Fryer, Isaac	
1711.	Fryer, Isaac	Antrim, Samuel	
1712.	Antrim, Samme	Turner, Henry (Capt.)	
1713.	Turner, Henry (Capt.)	Woodward, George	
1714.	Woodward, George	Tutman, Josiah	
1715.	Tutman, Josiah	Cook, John	
1716.	Cook, John	Sherwood, Henry	
1717.	Sherwood, Henry	Cole, Henry	
1718.	Cole, Henry	Goddard, William	Sarney, Thos. (Puttefor, Marmaduke, Beadle)
1719.	Goddard, William	Byland, John	
1720.	Byland, John	Lucas, James	
1721.	Lucas, James	Glover, John	
1722.	Glover, John	Vollett, David	
1723.	Vollett, David	Dan, John	
1724.	Dan, John	Davis, Ivan	
1725.	Davis, Ivan	Punter, Daniel	
1726.	Punter, Daniel	Brickley, William	

Year.	Master.	Upper Warden.	Clerk and Beadle.
1727.	Brickley, William	Parkins, Solomon	
1728.	Parkins, Solomon	Crawley, John	
1729.	Crawley, John	Bradford, Thomas	
1730.	Bradford, Thomas	Bray, Henry, and Tarbox, Joseph	
1731.	Bray, Henry	Harris, William	
1732.	Harris, William	Waldron, Brys	
1733.	Waldron, Brys	Tracy, John	
1734.	Tracy, John	Minns, Richard	
1735.	Minns, Richard	Young, Thomas	
1736.	Young, Thomas	Cooper, Joseph	
1737.	Cooper, Joseph	Shackleton, John	
1738.	Shackleton, John	Skipp, Thomas	
1739.	Skipp, Thomas	Corner, Charles	
1740.	Corner, Charles	Winterton, Thomas	
1741.	Winterton, Thomas	Young, Richard	
1742.	Young, Richard	Sharpe, John	
1743.	Sharpe, John	Taylor, William	
1744.	Taylor, William	Jarman, Mathew	
1745.	Jarman, Mathew	Pepiat, Thomas	
1746.	Pepiat, Thomas	Harford, John	
1747.	Harford, John	Smith, Thomas	
1748.	Smith, Thomas	Stowers, John	
1749.	Stowers, John	Harris, William (junr.)	(Wooton, John, *Beadle*)
1750.	Harris, William (junr.)	Dennis, Adam	(Lucas, Robert, *Beadle*)
1751.	Dennis, Adam	Greaves, John	
1752.	Greaves, John	Chanler, Francis	
1753.	Chanler, Francis	Ellis, Richard	
1754.	Ellis, Richard	Keene, William	
1755.	Keene, William	Lutton, Thomas	
1756.	Lutton, Thomas	Reckster, Samuel	Dann, senr., and Dann, Richard
1757.	Reckster, Samuel	Bosworth, John	
1758.	Bosworth, John	Gilman, Robert	
1759.	Gilman, Robert	Oake, Benjamin	
1760.	Oake, Benjamin	Chalfont, Peter	
1761.	Chalfont, Peter	Sharpe, William	
1762.	Hills, William	Hills, William	(Sucar, R., *Beadle*)
1763.	Sharpe, William	Lambert, Thomas	
1764.	Hare, Richard	Young, Lake	

Year.	Master.	Upper Warden.	Clerk and Beadle.
1765.	Lambert, Thomas	Tilton, John	(Skecorn, Peter, *Beadle*)
1766.	Young, Lake	Goodchild, Joseph	
1767.	Tilton, John	Mansell, William	
1768.	Goodchild, Joseph	Pulley, Joseph	
1769.	Mansell, William	Alexander, Edward	(Pontifex, William,
1770.	Pulley, Joseph	Pilon, Nicholas Peter	*Beadle*).
1771.	Alexander, Edward	Hanson, John	
1772.	Pilon, Peter Nicholas	Hanson, John	
1773.	Hanson, John	Hollyer, Richard	
1774.	Hollyer, Richard	Crawley, Gerard	
1775.	Crawley, Gerard	Willis, John	
1776.	Willis, John	Mowbray, James	(Croucher, Thomas,
1777.	Mowbray, James	Leachley, John	*Beadle*)
1778.	Leachley, John	Words, Richard	
1779.	Words, Richard	Alwinkle, Edward	
1780.	Alwinkle, Joseph	Ballard, Michael	Dann, Richard
			(Croucher, Thomas, *Bdle*.)
1781.	Ballard, Michael	Wright, William	
1782.	Wright, William	Graves, William	(Wilson, Benj., *Beadle*)
1783.	Graves, William	Smith, Edward	
1784.	Smith, Edward	Holmes, Thomas	
1785.	Holmes, Thomas	Hunt, Joseph	
1786.	Hunt, Joseph	Woods, John	
1787.	Woods, John	Dennis, Adam	
1788.	Dennis, Adam	Sedgwicke, Thomas	(Ward, Daniel, *Beadle*)
1789.	Sedgwicke, Thomas	Marson, W. Bosworth	(Buckland, ,,)
1790.	Marson, W. Bosworth	Hoare, Richard	
1791.	Hoare, Richard	Pulley, Joseph	
1792.	Pulley, Joseph	Green, John	
1793.	Green, John	Boardman, Joseph	
1794.	Boardman, Joseph	Allison, Charles	(Grument, Wm., *Beadle*)
1795.	Allison, Charles	Simpson, James	(Buckland, Joseph, ,,)
1796.	Simpson, James	Fenton, Thomas	
1797.	Fenton, Thomas	Stonard, John	Hindman,
1798.	Stonard, John	Hayward, Samuel	
1799.	Hayward, Samuel	Doull, Alexander	
1800.	Doull, Alexander	Thorogood, Samuel	
1801.	Thorogood, Samuel	Wheeler, Thomas	
1802.	Wheeler, Thomas	Fisher, William	
1803.	Fisher, William	Todd, George	

PERCY WILLIAM BERRIMAN TIPPETTS,
Clerk and Solicitor to the Company.

Year.	Master.	Upper Warden.	Clerk and Beadle.
1804.	Todd, George	Underwood, Francis	
1805.	Underwood, Francis	Marriott, John Martin	(Westall, Richd., *Beadle*)
1806.	Marriott, John Martin	Jaques, Richard	(White, Wm. „)
1807.	Jaques, Richard	Lovell, George	
1808.	Lovell, George	Barnes, Hector	
1809.	Barnes, Hector	Goodchild, Thomas	
1810.	Goodchild, Thomas	Skelton, William	
1811.	Skelton, William	Barnes, Hector	
1812.	Croucher, Thomas	Thorowgood,	
1813.	Croucher, Thomas	Thorowgood,	
1814.	Croucher, Thomas	Willis, John	
1815.	Willis, John	Cooke, Robert Alexander	
1816.	Cooke, Robt. Alexander	Jaques, William	
1817.	Cooke, Robt. Alexander	Boardman, Joseph (Junr.)	
1818.	Boardman, Joseph (Junr.)	Smith, Thomas Oak	J. Hindman,
1819.	Smith, Thomas Oak	Pabner, Thomas	
1820.	Pabner, Thomas	Brown, Thos.	
1821.	Brown, Thos.	Jones, Peter	
1822.	Jones, Peter	Armitage, John	
1823.	Armitage, John	Hoare, Richard	
1824.	Hoare, Richard	Banner, Henry	
1825.	Banner, Henry	Doyle, John	
1826.	Doyle, John	Henetson, Wm.	
1827.	Doyle, John	Fenton, Thos. Henry	
1828.	Crosfield, John Johnson	White, William	
1829.	Fenton, Thos. Henry	Crosfield, John Johnson	
1830.	White, William	Lovell, Wm.	
1831.	Lovell, Wm.	Goodchild, Thos.	
1832.	Lovell, Wm.	Lovell, Charles	
1833.	Lovell, Charles	Ainger, Nathaniel Lionel	
1834.	Ainger, Nathaniel Lionel	Peppercorn, Edward	
1835.	Young, Robert Kale	Peppercorn, Edward	
1836.	Peppercorn, Edward	Stonard, Samuel	J. J. Hindman,
1837.	Stonard, Samuel	Feversham, Mark	
1838.	Feversham, Mark	Boardman, Joseph	
1839.	Boardman, Joseph	Whiskin, James	
1840.	Whiskin, James	Goad, Charles	
1841.	Goad, Charles	Fenton, Thos. Henry	
1842.	Fenton, Thos. Henry	Lovell, William	

Year.	Master.	Upper Warden.	Clerk and Beadle.
1843.	Lovell, William	Lovell, Charles	Hindman,
			(Atkinson, *Beadle*)
1844.	Lovell, Charles	Ainger, Nathaniel Lionel	C. H. Lovell (*Clerk till*
1845.	Ainger, Nathaniel Lionel	Feversham, Mark	1884)
1846.	Feversham, Mark	Sherwin, Matthew Henry	
1847.	Sherwin, Matthew Henry	Ewing, Matthew	
1848.	Ewing, Matthew	Jones, Peter (junr.)	
1849.	Jones, Peter (junr.)	Buddrich, Geo. Washington	
1850.	Buddrich, Geo. Washington	Lovell, William J.	
1851.	Lovell, William J.	Ord, John	
1852.	Ord, John	Fenton, Thomas Joshua	
1853.	Fenton, Thomas John	Lovell, Charles	
1854.	Lovell, Charles (junr.)	Lovell, William	
1855.	Lovell, William	Young, John Toukin	
1856.	Young, John Tonkin	Whiskin, James Fuller	
1857.	Whiskin, Jas. Fuller	Ainger, N. L.	
1858.	Jones, Peter (junr.)	Buddrich, Geo. Washington	
1859.	Buddrich, J.	Trimby, James	
1860.	Trimby, James	Linton, James	
1861.	Linton, James	Lloyd, Thomas	
1862.	Lloyd, Thomas	Wainwright, Hy.	
1863.	Wainwright, Hy.	Lovell, Fredk. Geo.	
1864.	Lovell, F. G.	Hill, Henry	
1865.	Hill, Henry	Millington, Thomas A.	
1866.	Millington, Thomas A.	Fenton, T. J.	
1867.	Fenton, T. J.	Proctor, Robert	
1868.	Proctor, Robert	Trinby, James	
1869.	Trinby, James	Hill, Henry	
1870.	Hill, Henry	Millington, Thomas A.	
1871.	Millington, Thomas A.	Young, Antony	
1872.	Young, Antony	Wainwright, Wm.	
1873.	Wainwright, Wm.	Fenton, Thomas Joshua	
1874.	Fenton, T. Joshua	Proctor, Robert	
1875.	Fenton, T. Joshua	Cann, Charles	
1876.	Cann, Charles	Proctor, R. W.	Lovell, Thomas
1877.	Proctor, R. W.	Fendrick, Henry	(*Beadle till* 1909)
1878.	Fendrick, Henry	Courtney, William	
1879.	Fendrick, Henry	Courtney, William	
1880.	Courtney, William	Burgess. Jas. J.	

Year.	Master.	Upper Warden.	Clerk and Beadle.
1881.	Gravis, F. C.	Jones, F. W.	
1882.	Jones, Fredk. W.	Marsh, Wm. Robt.	
1883.	Wainwright, Wm.	Sturgis, R. O.	
1884.	Sturgis, Robt. Owen	Thornes, Geo. Thistle	Tippetts, James Berriman
1885.	Thornes, G. T.	Fenton, Chas. Enos	(*Clerk till* 1898)
1886.	Fenton, Chas. Enos.	Barnes, Thos. John	
1887.	Proctor, R. W.	Proctor, Robert W.	
1888.	Woodbridge, Stephen	Matthews, David	
1889.	Matthews, David	Green, Frank	
1890.	Green, Frank	Green, Samuel Love	
1891.	Green, Samuel Love	Green, Henry	
1892.	Green, Henry	Dodd, Grantham R.	
1893.	Dodd, Grantham R.	Sturgis, Robert Owen	
1894.	Sturgis, R. O.	Thornes, Geo. Thistle	
1895.	Thornes, Geo. Thistle	Twigg, W. James	
1896.	Twigg, W. James	Torkington, Abner	
1897.	Torkington, Abner	Tocher, Peter	
1898.	Woodbridge, Stephen	Fenton, Chas. Enos	Tippetts, W. J. Berriman
1899.	Fenton, Chas. Enos.	McGeagh, Benj. Scott F.	(*Clerk till* 1912)
1900.	McGeagh, Benj. Scott F.	Matthews, David	
1901.	Matthews, David	Gilling, Sydney	
1902.	Gilling, Sydney	Hewlitt, Chas. Fredk.	
1903.	Hewlitt, Chas. Fredk.	Walford, Geo. Paget	
1904.	*Walford, Geo. Paget	Colpoys, William	
1905.	Colpoys, William	Kennedy, John	
1906.	Kennedy, John	Green, Samuel Love	
1907.	Green, Samuel Love	Aufholz, August	
1908.	Aufholz, August	Reynolds, W. Foster	
1909.	Reynolds, W. Foster	Dyas, Robert	W. R. Skinner (*Beadle*)
1910.	Dyas, Robert	Edmunds, Henry	
1911.	Edmunds, Henry	Dyke, George	
1912.	Dyke, George	Wallace, Matthew	Percy W. B. Tippetts (*Clerk*)
1913.	Wallace, Matthew	Gilling, Sydney	
1914.	Charles Fredk. Hewlitt	Tippetts, W. J. Berriman	
1915.	Tippetts, W. J. Berriman	Walford, George Paget	
1916.	*Walford, George Paget (2nd time)	Foster, Harry Seymour	
1917.	*Walford, George Paget (3rd time)	Foster, Harry Seymour	
1918.	*Walford, George Paget (4th time)	Foster, Harry Seymour	Pittock, George Fredk. (*Beadle*)

*Master 1904, 1916, 1917, 1918—A unique honour.

RENTER WARDENS.

Owing to exigencies of space the Renter Wardens have not been included. As the Upper Warden of one year was generally the Renter Warden of the previous year their identification presents no difficulty. The exceptions are as follows :—

1727. Crawley, John, and Ragdell, John
1744. Hodson, Robert, and Pepiat, Thomas
1745. Harford, John, and Fitzwater, Richard
1750. Moore, William
1751. Corbin, John, and Thornton, Edward
1753. Hoare, William
1755. Pilon, William
1778. Alwinkle, Robert
1787. Robinson, John
1793. Bradshaw, —
1916-7-8. Grimwade, Charles Walter

Renter Warden:
CHARLES WALTER GRIMWADE, F.R.G.S.

CHAPTER IX.

THE CHARITIES.

HERE are four Charities administered by the Glaziers and Painters of Glass Company. These Charities are as follows :—

1.—*Abraham Wall's Charity.*

This was founded by the Will of Abraham Wall, Citizen and Glazier, whereby 40s. per annum was to be distributed unto four aged poor women of the Company, payable quarterly. The amount was previously secured by a rent-charge upon certain premises in Ironmonger Lane belonging to the Mercers' Company, but is now represented by a capital sum of £80 Two and a-half per cent. Stock standing in the name of the Official Trustee, who pays the Company the dividends quarterly in January, April, July and October.

2.—*Robert Taynton's Charity.*

This was founded by the Will of Robert Taynton, Citizen and Glazier, in 1679, whereby £5 per annum was to be paid for the relief of so many poor widows or decayed Freemen of the Company as they (the Company) should think fit, and not to be employed for any other purpose. The amount is derived from a rent-charge on No. 334, St. Margaret's Hill, Southwark (now No. 66, Borough High Street), and is now paid subject to a small deduction of land tax.

3.—*John Oliver's Charity.*

This was founded by the Will of John Oliver in 1699, whereby a sum of £3 per annum, payable by half-yearly payments, was to be distributed to three poor widows of the Company. The amount was previously secured by a rent-charge on No. 90, Queen Street, Cheapside, which was some years since acquired by the Corporation of London, who, desiring to free it from the rent-charge, redeemed it by the investment of £120 Consolidated Stock, which stands in the name of the Official Trustee, from whom are received the quarterly dividends in January, April, July and October.

4.—Vollett and Knight's Charity.

This originally consisted of two Trusts, which have for many years been merged.

Vollett's Charity was founded by his Will in 1724, and consisted of £3 per annum, payable by half-yearly payments for the use of the poor of the Company, and was derived from a rent-charge in Crown Court, Shoreditch, which he left to his daughter Elizabeth Knight.

Elizabeth Knight by her Will in 1728 gave the property to the Company, and the rents were to be divided among such poor Freemen or their widows as the Company should think fit, each of such to be paid 10s. The rent of the house, amounting to £19 11s. 8d. per annum, was received up to June, 1873, when the property was sold to the Metropolitan Board of Works for the net sum of £915 4s. 1d., which, by Order of the High Court, was invested in Consols, producing an income of £27 14s. 6d. In June, 1879, under another Order, the Consols were sold, and after paying expenses the nett amount was invested by the Company in the purchase of freehold ground rents which produce a profit rental of £37 16s. 0d.

CHAPTER X.

THE period covered by the Minute Book, 1697 to 1718, is undoubtedly one of the quaintest in English history, and the side-lights thrown upon the times by a perusal of the Records of the Meetings are of very considerable interest. The business done in the times of William and Mary by glaziers and painters of glass, clad in huge wigs and ample sleeves, broad brimmed hats and feathers, square-cut vests, lace ruffles and neckerchiefs, tight knee-breeches, stockings, and square-toed shoes, is as peculiar as their dress and as quaint as their language. With all their harshness and prompt haling of defaulters to prison, they have that touch of human nature which makes the whole world kin, and exhibit the greatest solicitude and forgiveness when requisite. Their respect for aged widows, pensioners, and the like, and the veneration they have for the ministers of religion all appear in their records, from which the salient features only have been transcribed, it being impossible to reproduce the whole.

The book is bound in ancient parchment sadly the worse for wear; the writing is uniformly good and legible—much in advance of the general caligraphy of the day. The Loriners' Hall episodes are very human, the bargaining and playing up for position very lifelike. With Queen Anne's accession there came to the Company apparently a time when feasting and revelry reigned supreme—when "entertainments" appeared to be part and parcel of civic life; when dignity and stateliness assumed the utmost importance with gentlemen glaziers in wire-distended coats and embroidered waistcoats, silk stockings, and square-toed, red-heeled shoes. The small three-cornered hat, laced with gold galloon, covered under its Kevenhuller cock, or Ramillies tilt, a painter of glass to whom even the Livery robe he wore was not sufficiently conducive to his dignity, and consequently it was ordered in Court that the Master and Wardens should provide " knotts," *i.e.*, rosettes and ribbons, still further to enhance his joyous appearance. It was apparently unkind of him to disallow women in the stands. Did he covertly harbour the conviction that he might be outshone, or that at least it might be a dangerous rivalry?—prevention undoubtedly is always better than cure !

The reader will be struck by the continued mention of prisons in the Minutes—even the Beadle himself was not immune from the talons of the law—and the conviction is gradually borne in upon the mind that to spend a certain portion of one's time in the quiet seclusion (or riotous surroundings) of Ludgate Prison was not only the usual method of life in that age, but had rather a sporting flavour about it. The non-payment of fines and dues to the Company seems to imply that debt was the chief cause for incarceration at that time.

An item which is strongly apparent also is the jealousy with which the Company guarded their feasts against possible criticisms of an unkind nature by forbidding the presence of ladies or apprentices, or anybody not specially invited. No doubt they were wise, for the days of Queen Anne were not those of the temperance reformer, and perhaps the sight of a venerable painter of glass revelling in his cups, or of a master Glazier under the table, did not make for good even in that tolerant age.

1697.—Court held 24. Jan. 1697, being the Convertion of St. Paul, there were present the Master, two Wardens and 14 Assistants. James Whelley the late apprentice of Richard Roades Cit. and Founder upon Test. of the said Mr Rodes made free and paid   -   -   -   -   -   -   -   -   -   -   -   £1   o   o

not enrolled   -   3   4

Ordered that enquiry be made after the Appce of Mr Winch who was bound in the Painters Comp. to the Beadle thereof.

Great in arrear for Quarterage [6 names]

Thomas Burgis struck his proof piece and paid   -   -   -   -   6   8

Ordered that Mr Nelmes (?) be warned before the Court of Consuce [Conscience ?] . . . . for the Twenty Shillings he oweth this Comp.

1697.—Feb. 5. Ordered that seuerall persons hereunder named shall have the Recorders Warrant served upon them for making light leads and non-payment of Quarterage [12 names].

1697.—Mch. 24. John Brush by trade Gunmaker . . . . made free by Patrimony. xxs.

1698.—Mar. 26. John Daldron having retained and kept John Skillman as an apprentice (over & besides the other he now hath) for about the space of six months contrary to the law of this Company in this behalfe and having submitted himself unto this Court. It is now Ordered, Declared and Agreed that hee the said Geo. Daldron for the said offence shall forfeit and pay unto this Company the sum of Thirty Shillings and being called into Court and acquainted therewith he freely paid down the same and this Court having seriously considered his case and submission returned him back 15s. of his said fine.

1698.—Ap. 28. Susanna Needham admitted into a Pension of 5s. a quarter in the room of Mary Batchelor, dec^d beginning at St. Peters Day next.

Ordered that 5s. apiece be given unto the Widow Wile and Widow Arnor and vnto Mr. Henry's daughter.

1698.—Sep. 19. A complaint was made this day against Joseph Gurney in Lower Shadwell for exercising the trade without right.

Ordered that Tenn Shillings be given unto Mr Samuel Griffiths, One of the Ministers of the Chamber, for his services to this Company.

Ordered that a Writt in the Court of King's Bench be served upon Wm Bennison for 54s. quarteridge at this Companys suite.

This day John Wotton was fined 2 . 6 for a light lead.

1698.—Nov. 18. Mr. Roland Watson paid in full of all Fines for defaulting Diuers appearants at Court to this day Tenn Shillings to the poores box.

Ordered that search be made for what Fines and Punishments have been laid upon Stewards which have not well performed their Duty in making their Feasts.

1699.—Ap. 25. Mr. J. Goodchild and Mr. Thos. Gurnett being in nominacon for an Assistant Mr. Job Harris being dec^d, and by majority of pricks the same Mr. J. Goodchild is chosen.

James Towers having worked with a light lead is ordered to be prosecuted for the same but afterwards submitted himself and paid - - - - *2s. 6d.*

1699.—May 2. Ordered that the paper now read concerning Masters, Journeymen and Vicemaker be forthwith printed to the No. of 2000 at the cost of the Company.

1699.—Oct. 5. Richard Powell who was lately chosen one of the Stewards of the Company appeared and prayed to be excused, But this Court Believing him to be of ability have Fined him for refusing to hold the said office Six Pounds being the ancient fine for the same.

Ordered that the Clerk of this Company may give copies of the Charter and Bye laws of this Company to any person who may desire the same.

1699.—22 Oct. E. Clerk is hereby chosen one other Steward for this present year and being acquainted therewith pretended inability but this Court believing him to be of good ability is resolved he shall be summoned before the Lord Maior for such his refusall.

Ordered that Thomas Hyatt be made Free in this Company by Virtue of an Act of Parliament made in the Tenth and Eleventh Years of K. William the Third in Faviour of such as have served his Majesty in his warrs at any time Since his accession to ye Throne at the discreĉōn of the Master and Wardens for the time being.

1700.—Sep. 26.   The Clerk and Beadle continued for a year.

1700.—Oct. 29.   Richard Say Son of Robert Say late of Doncaster in ye County of York Musition dec^d doth put himself apptce. to Lettice Good Widow relict of ffrancis Good dec^d for 7 yeares -   -   -   -   -   -   -   -   2 . 6.

1701.—Jan. 29.   The Glaziers Company was Joyned with the ffishmongers and others for their proporĉōn of land in Ireland and paid in £32 to the first purchase as appears at ye Comon Councell held ye 17. Dec. 1613   Informed Mr Thompson 22 July 1678 at ye Bell in Nicholas Lane for Mr Kerrie Cheife Agent in London Derry.   [55 Companies lent £40,000.]

1702.—Ap. 25.   Ordered that the Master and Wardens . . . . shall make further search concerning the monies lent by this Company for certain lands in Ireland and to do therein as the said Committee shall think fit & to make report thereof to this Court.

1702.—May 6.   A Subpenæ taken out of the Exchequer against Thomas Osborne Returneable the fifth of June next being the first day of Trinity Terme.

1702.—Nov. 30.   Ordered that the Renter Warden do pay and bestow forty shillings in case that Sum will discharge Thomas Stacey from Leidgate Prison and not otherwise.

1703.—Ap. 26.   Ordered that the M^r and Ward^ns do prosecute in the Court of Exchequer or other Court such Members as owe Quarteriage according to ye discretōn of ye Master and Wardens.

1703.—Sept. 21.   Ordered that the Suite against William While for working in the City being an unfreeman shall be further prosecuted.

The names of the severall Walkes used by this Company at goeing their Search within vizt :

North Walke within	South within London
Criplegate	Southwarke and
Holborne	Wapping
Westminster	

1704.—July 1.   Henry Ferele the late apprentice of William Cox since deceased made free sworne and paid 3s. 4d.   Margaret Cox Widdow Relict and Administratrix Repourter.

Memorand.   That Abraham Harris Beadle of this Company departed this life on Tuesday the 29th August 1704 about [blank] in the evening.

1704.—Sept. 4. Ordered that complyance be given to the Lord Mair's Precepts for recepton of her Maʸ at her passage to St. Pauls on Thursday the 7th inst. by the Assistants and Livery of this Company and that an Entertainment of Victualls be provided for the Livery and Assistants of the Company at the discreton of the Maʳ and Wardens.

1704.—Sep. 21. Gilbert Brandon continued Clerke for the year ensuing.

Ordered that all such who have past the Office of Steward shall be admitted into the Livery except John Wotton William Weale Robert Walker and that they be summoned to a Court on Wednesday next at 2 afternoon.

1704.—Oct. 19. This day was delivered unto the Stewards and each of them a Bill of ffare who promised punctually to pforme the same which Bill of ffare was in the following Termes. [The " termes " are unfortunately not given.]

1705.—June 29. Ordered that John Gulling shall be prosecuted for non-payment of his Quarterage and for working a light lead according to the discretion of the Master and Wardens and as they shall be advised also for not striking out their proof peices.

That yᵉ Search shall be on Tuesday Seuen night next.

1705.—At a Speciall Court Holden for the Said Company on Thursday 23 of August 1705 and there present [14 names given].

No other business than attending on their glands [! !]

1705.—Sep. 21. At this Court Charles Scrivens fforreigner was fined for alight lead and paid - - - - - - - - - - - - 5s. 0d.

Ordered that Thomas Stacey yᵉ Beadle do bind an Apprenᵉ for Henry ffoule and take security in £50 for indempnity for all accidents and to turn him over to him when he shall be qualified to take an apprentice.

1706.—June 26. On Thursday ribans shall be provided for this Company against ye aforesaid day for to hold yᵉ Colours by and a dinner if it may be had conveniently at yᵉ Cooks and that all ornaments be provided for yᵉ entertainment of his Majestie as yᵉ Precept directs musick excepted.

1706.—Oct. 14. Also that the Clerke do goe to the Master of the Loriners Company and know of him what terms they can grant this Company for their continuance in this Hall.

1706.—Oct. 29. Yesterday Gilbert Brandon Clerke of this Company (By Order) did deliver unto Thomas Stay [?] now Beedle of his Company the Charter and By-Lawes of this Company in good order and Condicon in order to have the same deposited and safely kept in a chest now at Loriners' Hall for this Companies use provided and kept.

1706.—27 Dec. At this Court it is ordered and directed that the Maʳ and Wardens at the costs of this Company shall and cause Stands to be Erected and provide a fitting Entertainmᵗ for the Assistants and Livery of this Company with due attendants on the 31st of this instant December being a Day of Generall Thanks-giveing appointed by Her Majesty's Proclamacōn psuant to a precept from the Lord Maior dated the 23rd inst. and what else shall be thought necessary as Knotts, Ribbons, &c.

1706.—Ap. 25.   That in case the Lord Maior's precept Do require this Companies publick appearance on Thursday next Then the Maʳ and Wardens at their discretion shall make befitting entertainment for this Company with what else shall be needful for such an Occasion.

At a Court holden for this Company on Thursday 1st May 1707, being Thanks-giving Day for yᵉ Union Betwixt England and Scotland this Court with many of the Livery of this Company marched from their Hall to their Stands appointed them for the more splendid Recepcōn of Her most gracious Queen Anne in Her passage to St. Paul's Church on this Occasion.

1707.—May 10.   It is Ordered and Directed that on Wednesday the 13ᵗʰ of this instant May a General Search in and amongst the Glaziers shall begin and be made by the persons following vizt.

> North Walke within the City [3 names, including the Master and the Clerk].
> Cripplegate [3 names].   Holborn Walk [3 names].
> Westminster Walk [3 names, including the Upper Warden].
> South Walk within London [3 names, including the Renter Warden].
> Southwark Walk [3 names].   Wapping Walk [2 names, and the Beadle].

1707.—June 30.   Ordered that at the Costs of this Company a fitt and decent new Gowne be provided for the use of the Beedle in the service of this Company according to the discrecōn of the Maʳ and Wardens.

1707.—Oct. 29.   This Court have ordered their Beadle to arrest George Weller as a foreigner.

1708.—May 20.   [At a Walk upon this date those for the South Walke met at Gurnetts Coffee House; for the North Walk at the Coffee House agt. Mr. Lucas in Warwick Lane, at 6 in the morning.]

1708.—June 29.   Also Mr. John Cooke and Mr. Henry Sherwood being in nominacōn for an Assistant now vacant by the Removall of George Bradford for great mis-demeanors hee the said Mr. John Cooke is hereby Chosen accordingly.   And it is hereby further ordered that the name of the said George Bradford be struck out of the Assistants Roll and placed on the Livery Role.

1708.—Aug. 19.   At a Courte holden for the said Companey on Thursday yˢ 19th Aug. 1708 being a Day of Publick Thanksgiving for a Victory obtained over yᵉ French at [no place given, but it was undoubtedly the Battle of Oudenarde, fought on July 11].

1708.—Oct. 22.   Ordered that a ffines Gowne be forthwith provided at the Costs of this Company to be worn by the Maʳ of this Company for the time being on publick daies.

1709.—Ap. 21. Ordered that the Master and Wardens are hereby authorized to consider of wayes and meanes to promote the welfare and Interest of the glazeing trade and to make Report thereof unto this Court.

1709.—May 26. Rules and Methods to be observed by all the Members of this Company as often as they shall be requested to Value any Glazeing Worke In not setting thereon any lower or lesser rates or prices than is hereunder particularly menc̄oned and Limitted viz.—

Per Ffoot and not under [all details are omitted].

1709.—Sep. 9. Friday the 9th Sep. 1709.

This day the Clerke of this Company did take over of the Court of Exchequer a writt returnable the first day of Michaelmas Terme at the Suite of this Company for refusing payment of Quarterage mony against the follg persons [the names given are Thomas Brettle, Edward Wall, and John Wright. The original writ, dated 13 July, 8 Anne (1709), is in possession of the Company].

This day a Labell was left for the said Mr. Wright [one of the three preceding] who imediately after acknowledged the same and promised to submitt to the Company. [He owed 54 Quarterages.]

1710.—Ap. 13. It is likewise ordered yt the 40s. remaining with Mr. Luttman and yt of his expenses 20s. more so yt it do not exceed those sums This Court will allow it provided it will release Mr. Carr out of prison & send him to sea.

1710.—Oct. 17. Ordered that no apprentices or servants shall be in the Hall at Dinner Time on the Lord Mayors Day next in the forfeiture of 2s. 6d. for every one so offending.

1710.—Nov. 17. Ordered that New List of the Court as they stood on the Lord Mayors day last be written in Parchment.

1710.—Jan. 25. And it is hereby further ordered and agreed that no Assistants wifes shall be at Dinner with this Company but on St. Matthews Day onely being the Eleac̄on for Mar and Wardens of this Company And that none other than the Assistants and the proper Officers shall Dine on the other quarter Dayes excepting such as the Master and Wardens shall invite and that none of the Livery shall be permitted to dine on any of the Quarter Dayes untill they shall first pay down twelvepence apiece.

1711. Feb. 29. Daniell Daviellson in petty France Westminster to be summoned to show at the next Court what right he hath to the Glazing Trade.

1711.—Oct. 29. It is ordered ye Renter Warden pay ye £16 owing at ye Queen's Arm's Tavern and fetch away ye Master's best gown left there by ye Beadle.

It is also ordered ye following psons. yt did not attend going to ye Stands be sumoned at ye next Court vizt :

Assistants [5 names].
Livery [27 names].

1711.—Jan. 20.   Ordered that Ten Shillings be given for William Weele's discharge from Ludgate Prison.

1712.—Sep. 22.   A complaint ag. Margaret Hamilton for keeping a Shop in the Liberty of London being unfree & ordered to be arrested if she continues.

A Search was made on Tuesday May 4, 1714 to meet at Tart's Coffee House in Warwick Lane at Seven in the morning.   [The last is an insert pinned in the book with a contemporary pin.]

1713.—June 19.   It is ordered that the Master & Wardens at their discreĉon shall make an Entertainment for this Company on the 7th July next being appointed for a General Thanksgiveing in case a precept from the Lord Maior shall be sent unto this Company in their behalf . . . .   No women to be in the Stands and all the Members to appear in Gowns.

And that any sum of money not exceeding 40 Shillings be advanced for obtaining the Beadle's Liberty from Ludgate Prison to attend on this Companies affairs.

1714.—At a Court specially held for yᵉ sd. Company for their attendance as his Majesty makes his Royal procession through yᵉ Citty of London to his Royal Palace at St. James on Monday the 20ᵗʰ day of September (Pursuant to yᵉ Lord Mayor's Precept & order).

1715.—Oct. 4.   Wᵐ Orton in Long Alley near the Dolphin (in Moorfield) chosen Steward and refuseing to appear and accept thereof is to be sumoned before the Lord Mayor to meet at ye "Woolpack" in ffosse Lane on Friday next at 9 in ye morning agt. wh. time ye sᵈ 2 persons to be sumoned.

1715.—Oct. 29.   Mem. Mʳ Snead did not pay ye Clks. & Beadle's fees on his Cloathing (Since pd.).

1715.—Jan. 25.   Ordered that a lease be granted to Mʳ William Broxill of the Houses in Queene Street . . . .

1716.—Dec. 14.   Elizabeth Halsey daughter of Thomas Halsey of London Gent. doth put herself apprentice unto Elizabeth Daldron Citizen and Glazier of London for 7 yeares and paid   -   -   -   -   -   -   -   -   -   -   2 - 6.

1717.—Oct. 2.   Ordered that ye Maʳ and . . . . be a Comittee to treat with ye Company of Loriners for a lease for yᵉ use of yᵉ Hall and appurtᶜᵉˢ the Comp. of Glaziers now hold & to meet at yᵉ Feathers Taverne in Cheapside on Thursday yᵉ 10th inst. at 3 in yᵉ Afternoon.

1717.—Jan. 14.   [Lease to Mr Wᵐ Broxall of 4 houses in Great Queen Street London for 18 years.]

1717.—Feb. 22.   This day the Warden and others attended the Company of Loriners who acquainted them that they would not grant this Companye a Lease of their Hall upon the terms lately proposed by the Company   But did come to this resolution that a Lease should be granted the Company of the premises for Twenty yeares from Christmas next with the Lord Mayor's Day inclusive at £50 fine and

£20 per annum rent, Or exclusive of the Lord Mayor's Day at £50 fine and £8 per annum rent and would come to no other resolution   Whereupon a Court of Assistants is appointed for this Company to be held on Tuesday the 11 of March next at 3 in the Afternoon to make Report hereof.

1717.—Mar. 11.   The Court deferred giving their answer to ye Loriners' Company resolucõn till next qter. Court Day.

1718.—Ap. 9.   Upon ye petn of sevll psons for Beadles place in room of Thos. Sarny Decd Marmaduke Puttefor was chose and sworne.

1718.—Oct. 2.   Ordered that they propose to take the lease of Lorrinors Hall for 20 years from Xmas. next at £25 fine and £10 per ann. rent ye Lord Mayor's Day included or else at ye same fine and at £8 per ann. for ye sd. term exclusive of ye Lord Mayor's Day and to acquaint ye Mar of Ye Lorriners Company therewith forthwith.   The Committee retd. and brot. this Answer That ye Lorriners Company would not agree to above proposalls and yt ye Company of Glaziers doe forthwith remove from ye Hall unless they did pay £50 fine and £10 per ann. rent ye Lord Mayors Day included.

1718.—Oct. 7.   Ordered and agreed that the Mar and one Warden shall agree with the Comp of Lorriners for the use of their Hall with all the privileges they now hold for about the terme of nineteen yeares at £50 fine and £10 per ann. by lease with the same Covenants contained in the Lease lately granted by the said Company of Lorinors if they will not abate any thing of the said Rent and Fine and that the Lord Mayor's Day be included with the daies to be granted this Company as in the former lease.

1718.—Oct. 9.   This day the Lorinors Company agreed to grant a lease unto this Company of the use of their Hall with all of the said privileges this Company now have and formerly granted them for 20 years from Xmas last at £40 fine and £10 rent and order to such effect.   [The Lease was signed Jan. 13th, 1718, and is copied out in full in the Minutes.   It appears that the Glaziers used the Hall for eighteen days in every year, giving due notice to the Loriners' Company when they required it.]

The Minute Book 1742 to 1760 ; reign of Geo. II.

The chief points of interest respecting the Company of Glaziers and Painters of Glass dealt with in this Minute Book are those relating to Loriners' Hall, which was in use for the whole of the period covered for the purpose of holding the chief meetings of the Company.   There is no actual mention of any disagreements between the Glaziers and the Loriners respecting the Hall, but the abrupt manner in which the decision not to renew the lease is recorded seems to point to the fact that the Glaziers were not entirely comfortable in those quarters.   The nuisance as to smells, etc., emanating from the kitchen is significant of the last suggestion inasmuch as the Loriners made the Company pay for the measures taken to abate the nuisance.

But the chief event prominent in the Glaziers' Annals is the set of By-Laws of 1749, and their production, because they are those which now regulate the Company.   The care and attention devoted to their compilation is very evident from the Minutes, and we may freely forgive them for being both hungry and thirsty after arduous work upon their production.   The full text of these By-Laws are preserved in the Company's records.   (*See* page 130).

The South Sea Stock purchased by the Company is of interest because it manifests to a certain degree the spirit of speculation rife in that age which, although the Bubble had burst and ruined many thousands years before, still held the public in its grip and caused an uncontrollable fascination by its very name.   It is only fair to add, however, that the New Stock lacked much of the gambling element so characteristic of the old.

The places of meeting, apart from Loriners' Hall, have been carefully preserved by the author, inasmuch as the localities of the old Inns, Taverns, and Coffee Houses of London exercise a fascination for many people who are interested in their ichnography, and a chance allusion in a work like the present may possibly determine a disputed point.

1742.—Nov. 30. [Meeting held in Loriners' Hall.]

1743.—Aug. 24. At the House of Mr. William Benford the sign of the Mermaid in Houndsditch, London.

1743.—June 29. Ad huc Court.

1743.—Sept. 28. As Yet Court.

1743.—Oct. 13. Mr. Samuel Chandler attended and desired that the Court would not insist on his taking upon him the office of Assistant of this Company for that he apprehended himself to be excused by virtue of the Act of William & Mary for Toleration as a Dissenting Minister.   But in regard of preserving Peace he would present the Company with the sum of Eight Guineas. [Excused.]

1743.—Nov. 30. Ordered that Mr. Matthew Jarman do buy £50 South Sea New Annuity Stock out of the Company's cash.

1744.—Nov. 30. Order that Mr. Thomas Pegriat do (if he thinks fit) buy £50 New South Sea Annuity Stock.

1745.—Sep. 21. Ordered that it be proposed on the behalf of this Company to the Company of Loriners that if the said Company will sash their Great Hall this Company will provide Crown Glass and glaze the said sashes, or that if the said Company of Loriners rather choose to have those windows continue as they are this Company will glaze them with Crown Glass and large squares and strong lead, provided the said Company of Loriners will make new Casements.

1745.—Sept. 21. Ordered that Mr. Waldron do provide musick to attend this Company on the next Lord Mayor's Oath Day.

1745.—Oct. 29. Ordered that a Copper Plate with this Company's Arms fairly engraved thereon be gotten by the Renter Warden for the use of this Company and also one pair of small Waxlight Candlesticks of White Metal with the Company's Arms engraven handsomely on them for the Use of this Court at their several Meetings.

1745.—Jan. 25. Whereas the Master and Wardens of this Company did heretofore use to go to and amongst the several Glaziers and Painters of Glass inhabiting within the City of London and three miles thereof to search view try and oversee their works according to the power to them given in this Company's Charter of Incorporation whereby many deceits and abuses are prevented which Custom hath been for some years past discontinued. It is therefore ordered that the same be now again revived as heretofore hath been accustomed.

1746.—Sept. 2. Ordered that for the future Musick shall always be provided to attend this Company on every Lord Mayor's Day to consist of one Trumpet 3 Hautboys and one Bassoon and that this Company will pay and allow for the said Musick the sum of £5. 15. 6.

1746.—Nov. 26. Ordered that the Renter Warden do transfer the £100 S.S.N. Annuity Stock which he hath in his Name in trust for this Company And that all Stock hereafter to be purchased be transferred to this Company in their Name of Incorporation.

1746.—Dec. 1. Ordered that the present Renter Warden do purchase £100 South Sea New Annuity Stock out of the Cash of this Company now in his hands.

1747.—June 29. At the House of Mrs. Elizabeth Danse (the sign of the Blew Ball) in Gracechurch Street London 13 Aug. 1747. By Order.

Bound. Mary Apps Daughter of Thomas late of Cranbrook in the County of to Kent Glasier dec^d· for 7 years by Indre Elizabeth Dans widow dated above. of Joell Dans late Citizen & Glasier of London decd.

1747.—Oct. 27. Att the Cock Ale House in Bell Alley Coleman Street. [A meeting held.]

1747.—Nov. 30 at 8 o'clock a.m.

Ordered that the present Renter Warden do purchase £50 South Sea New Annuity Stock . . . , and also that he do purchase two other Wax Candlesticks of Silver for the use of this Company of the same Pattern and Weight with those the Company already have.

1747.—Dec. 3.   At the Queen Head Tavern next Gray's Inn Gate in Holborn.   [A meeting held.]

1747.—Jan. 26.   At North's Coffee House in Kings Street Cheapside.   [A meeting held ; in the account of subsequent meetings it is added "near Guildhall."]

1747.—Feb. 27.   Att the House of Mr. John Stowers the renter Warden in Salisbury Court, Fleet Street.   [A meeting held.]

1747.—Mch. 3.   Att the House of Mr. Jarman the Master on Bread Street Hill, London.   [A meeting held.]

[In a book preserved in the Guildhall and published in the year 1747, it states that the Glaziers' Company then stood No. 53 in order of precedency, the Glass Sellers being 77th.   The Company possessed no Hall, but had a stand in Cheapside in which they sat to attend the Lord Mayor on the day of his installation.   Incidentally it mentions also that apprentices worked from 6 a.m. to 8 p.m., and that the wages of a journeyman glazier were from 12s. to 15s. per week.]

1748.—Ap. 25.   Ordered that the Renter Warden do buy two Table Cloths of 6 yards long and two yards wide each for the Court Room table.   [*Note* in Margin.—The table is 5 yards 2 inches long.]

1748.—Oct. 29.   Ordered that at All Courts of Assistants to be held for this Company (the Quarter Day Courts excepted) the sum of Twenty Shillings be paid out of this Company's Cash unto and divided equally among all and even the Assistants who shall appear within the time and space of one Hour next after the time mentioned in the Sumons for holding such Court at the place where the same is to be held   And that the Expiration of such Hour be determined by the Watch of the Master, Warden or Deputy Master or such of them as shall be then present and that each person not appearing as aforesaid do pay one shilling and that the Beadle do give notice of this Order to all the Ass^ts.

Ordered by this Court (by and with the approbation and consent of all the liverymen present) That a New Set of By-Laws for this Company be prepared and that Heads thereof be drawn up by the Clerk and laid before this Court on the Audit Day.

1748.—Nov. 30.   Ordered that a Court of Assistants of this Company be sumoned to meet at Loriners' Hall London on Thursday the 8th day of December next at Ten of the Clock in the forenoon to consult about the New By-Laws ; and because the same may very probably take up a great deal of time It is therefore Ordered That something be provided for the refreshment of the Assistants and to dine at Two of the Clock.

1748.—Dec. 8. The Heads for the drawing up of a new Sett of By-Laws were laid before the Court and the Court began to consider them and some progress were made therein and Ordered that a Court of Assistants of this Company be sumoned to meet at Loriners' Hall the 15th Day of December instant to confer further of the same at 10 of the Clock in the forenoon and that some refreshment be provided for the Assistants who shall attend at the Black Swan Tavern in Bartholomew Lane and to dine at 2 of the Clock.

1748.—Jan. 25. At this Court the Draught of the New By-Laws was laid before the Court and it is ordered that a Court of Assistants of this Company be sumoned to meet at the Black Swan Tavern in Bartholomew Lane near the Royal Exchange London on Monday the 2nd day of ffeby. next at 9 of the clock in the forenoon to read over and consider the said New By-Laws.

1748.—Feb. 2. Ordered that at every Quarter Day Court breakfast shall be sett on the Table exactly at 10 of the Clock and that everything relating thereto be removed and the Table cleared at 11 of the clock presicely so that Business may be and shall not be proceeded upon without hindrance or obstruction.

The Draught of the New By-Laws was now read and fully maturely and deliberately considered on by the Court and after some few alterations made therein was agreed to by the Court And it is Ordered That the same be again fairly copied and be forthwith laid before some Councill for his perusal and By-laws was considered and it was resolved that the Renter Warden for the time being do advance and lay out all such sums of money as shall be necessary for that and other purposes relating to the said By-Laws.

1749.—Ap. 4. Court of Assistants held at Blackwell's Coffee House in Well Court in Queen Street near Cheapside London.

The Master acquainted the Court that the reason of his calling them together at this time was to inform them of the Death of John Wootton late Beadle of this Company whereby the said office of Beadle is become vacant.

Ordered that as the Day of Public Thanksgiving on account of the Peace lately concluded [*i.e.,* the Peace of Aix-la-Chapelle] is appointed to be on the Feast of St. Mark the Evangelist being the 25th day of this Instant April therefore the Quarter Day Court of Assistants of this Company shall be held on the 26th day of this Instant April . . . at 9 o'clock and that a Dinner be provided for the Court at Loriners' Hall.

1749.—Ap. 26. At this Court Robert Lucas one of the Assistants of this Company desired to be a candidate for the office of Beadle and being withdrawn he was called in again and acquainted by the Master by Order of the Court That if he should be elected Beadle of this Company he must at all times behave courteously and obligingly to all the Assistants and in all things as a Beadle ought to do although he is now an Assistant and at all Courts attend without the Door unless called in and then to stay no longer than was necessary and then depart, and be diligent in collecting the Quarterage of the several Members &c.

Ordered that 1000 Copies of the Abstract of the Act of Common Councill made in Favour of this Company be printed and dispersed by the Beadle to every Glazier's Shop in London and the Liberties and also be given to every person that shall be Free of this Company and to every Glazier whose House, Shop, or Workplace shall be searched.

1749.—June 29. Ordered that whenever a search shall be made pursuant to this Company's Charter That 2s. 6d. be allowed for the expenses of each Assistant attending not exceeding 4 Assistants to each Walk and that the Beadle be paid 2s. 6d. for his trouble and attendance and also have his keeping.

Ordered that the old gowns of the Master and Wardens be given to the Beadle. [18 Assistants attended this Court and 20 the next against an average of less than 4 previously to payment being introduced.]

1749.—Oct. 30. Ordered that a new Gown be provided for the Beadle of this Company and that he do attend for the future every Court of Assistants in his Gown and that a Robemaker be desired to attend at the next Court and to bring with him patterns of several sorts and kinds of Beadle's gowns that the Court may choose one.

1749.—Nov. 30. Ordered that the Master Wardens and Deputy Master of this Company do and shall in conjunction consult and order the Bill of Fare and all other Matters and things whatsoever relating to and concerning the Two Several Dinners & Entertainment to be made and provided yearly—and that there shall be allowed them yearly for their charges and expenses about & concerning each of the said dinners the sum of £1 and no more.

1749.—Jan. 25. The Robemaker attended and brought the Beadle's New Gown and the Shag facing was disliked and ordered to be changed for the very best Shag wch can be gotten & that aft^wds he be paid £6.4.0 for the gown. [Shag, *i.e.*, Cloth with a rough nap.]

1749.—May 19. At this Court the Committee appointed to forward the new Bye Laws .... delivered in their Report in writing which was read and ordered to be entered in the Minute Book. The New By-Laws were read over to the Court with the alteration made thereto by the two Lords Chief Justices & the same were allowed approved & confirmed And It is Ordered that the same shall be forthwith Engrossed Fair in a German Text Hand on Vellum and afterwards bound in a book covered with Morocco Leather and Mr. John Holt Stationer attending received directions from the Court for that purpose. [This Copy is in possession of the Company.]

1749.—Mar. 9. Att Poole Coffee House without Bishopsgate London. [A meeting held.]

1750.—May 31. At this Court the New By-Laws having been fairly engrossed in a Book for that Purpose were signed by all the Assistants present and ordered that they be laid before the Chancellor and the Chief Justices for their Confirmation.

1750.—Aug. 9. [In the Report of this Court Loriners' Hall is stated to be near Fore Street.]

Ordered that a New Wainscot Box to keep the Plate, &c., with a drawer underneath to keep the Book of the Original New By-Laws.

Ordered that a Book be provided wherein the Beadle is to enter all apprentices bound to Glasiers.

1750.—Aug. 9. [At this Court regulations were made respecting the fees paid to the Clerk & the Beadle when Assistants & Livery men were admitted.]

Mr. John Holt sent his Bill about the New By-Laws amounting to £16.19.0 and he is to attend at next Court.

1750.—Sep. 21. Ordered that the Master Wardens and Deputy Master do consult with Mr. Crump about the Order for Glasiers to be made Free of this Company and make Report at next Court.

Ordered that a Copy of the Act of Comͦon Councill of 31st Oct. 14 K. James I. be had out of the Town Cl. Office.

1750.—Sep. 27. The Committee reported that they had met Mr. Crump and had procured a Copy of the Order of the Court made 9 May 1671.

That all Persons using Glasing be admitted in the Company of Glasiers only and the same was read and Ordered That 500 Copies of it be printed and given to all Glasiers and left with the several Companies of the City.

Mr. Wm. White being greviously afflicted with the Dead Palsy is excused from being elected to the Office of Renter Warden.

1750.—Oct. 29. Ordered that for the Future this Court do dine at the Hall on the Audit Day and that the Dinner to be provided on that day be always Two Hind Quarters of Lamb one Peice of Beef roasted and Two Dishes of Minced Pyes.

1750.—Nov. 30. Robert Street was at this Court chosen Cook to this Company during Good Behaviour. [A marginal note says " Chop Cook."]

1750.—Dec. 12. At the George Tavern in Ironmonger Lane London. [A Court held.]

1751.—June 29. Ordered that a suit be commenced against Richard Timberley and — Collingbourn Non-Freemen for working in the City of London.

1752.—Sep. 21. Ordered that another Coffee Pot be provided for the use of this Company larger than thei the Company now have.

Resolved that a New Set of Colours be provided for use of this Company.

Ordered that the Company of Loriners be desired to give orders that something be done to prevent the offensive smells and smoak arising out of the Kitchen under the Court Room and annoying the Company sitting therein. [This offence was subsequently obviated by the removal of stoves to another place in the kitchen, the part cost to the Glaziers being £4. 7. 2.]

1752.—Dec. 14. [A contribution of £5 towards the charities of the Company was received from the " Society of Cocknies."]

1753.—Jan. 25.   Mr. Richard Nash, painter, Attended and Agreed to paint a New Set of Colours viz. Two Streamers and one Standard in good and workmanlike manner for the sum of £22 (but the Silk fringe and making them are not to be included in the sum).

1753.—June 29.   Ordered that if any Member of this Company shall profanely curse or swear in the room where the Court of Assistants meet to do business such Member shall forfeit and pay for every such offence to the use of the Poor of this Company the summ of one Shilling.

Ordered that Pewter be provided and that the Renter Warden do consult with the Cook as to what quantity and what kind will be necessary & that such engraving be put on it as the Renter Warden shall think fit.

1754.—Feb. 25.   [Meeting held at the " White Hart," Golden Lane.]
Ordered that Ralph Bitter, &c., be summoned into the Court of Conscience for their Quarterage & that the Beadle do attend the Warden in so doing.

1754.—Nov. 30.   Agreed with William Perkinson for cleaning the Branch in the Hall, the Candlesticks Coffee Potts and other Utensils of the like kind for the sum of Ten Shillings by the year.

1755.—Feb. 13.   [Meeting held at the Paul's Head, Cateaton Street.]
Ordered that Thomas Perry be one of the Porters to Carry a Streamer on every Lord Mayor's Day.

1756.—June 29.   At this Court Richard Dann was chosen Clerk in the Room of his late Father.

1758.—Jan. 25.   Mr. Gilman reported that the Committee appointed to take a survey of the Company's Estate in Queen Street let on lease to Mrs. Ward and were of opinion that the said Houses might be let on a repairing lease for 21 years.   [The lease was granted at £30 per ann.]

1759.—Jan. 25.   Agreed that Capt. Harris be allowed Seven Pounds per annum to put up and take down and keep in repair for 7 years The Stand belonging to this Company, but if it should require a new Covering the same to be provided at the Expence of this Company.

1759.—Jan. 29.   Ordered that for the future no liveryman be permitted to bring any children on the Lord Mayor's Day.

1759.—Sep. 21.   [A Quarterly Court held at the Half Moon Tavern in Cheapside.]
Resolved that this Company do quit Loriners Hall at the expiration of their lease.
That this Company do hold their Courts at this Place [i.e., Half-Moon Tavern] until further notice.
Resolved that the following goods belonging to this Company be disposed of, viz. :—

14 Stone Muggs	A leaf Wainscot Table
6 doz. Glasses	4 long Forms
3 Earthern Plates	3 Leaves
2 Toasting Forks	5 Treffells
2 Bread Basketts	One cover to the Window Binn

3 Scriptured peices in Frames

Resolved that the following Goods belonging to this Company be kept at this Place, viz. :—

18 doz. Plates
15 Raisors for Fruit
12 Salts
18 Pye Plates
72 Dishes viz. 8, 16, 15 & 44
40 Butter Boats
3 doz. of Spoons
2 doz. of Brass Candlesticks
6 doz. for Tapers
6 pairs of Brass Snuffers and Stands
3 Coffee Potts
1 Copper Tea Kettle and Stand
2 Copper Drinking Potts
12 Coffee Cups
2 Sugar Dishes with Covers
2 Milk Potts
2 Tea Boards
4 Glasses with Frames
4 Search Boxes, Weights & Scales

1 Chest containing the Company's Charters old and new ByLaws, sundry old Deeds, Leases
19 Minute Books bound in parchment
Bills
A Bell
A Hammer
A Proofpiece Board
Quarterage Books
A Livery Gown
The Streamers
Abstracts of the Bye Laws
Acts of Common Councell
Beadles Gown & Staff
One other Chest
8 doz. Knives
A chest for the candlesticks
The pewter with the Company's Arms

A foldend Cupboard with the Bye Laws and a green Cloth.

1757.—Oct. 4. Resolved that there be only 2 boys on the Lord Mayor's Day to bear the Streamers.

1759.—Nov. 30. [At this Court the Company owed the Renter Warden the sum of £49. 15. 4.]

1760.—Jan. 25. Resolved that for the future this Company be summoned to meet at their Courts at 9 of the clock in the Forenoon and that the Court do breakfast together & proceed to Business at 10 of the clock exactly.

1760.—June 30. The Court taking into consideration the State of the Company's Affairs Resolved That a General Dinner of Assistants and of Liverymen on St. Matthew's Day be put off this year.

Minute Book 1761 to 1779.

1761.—Queen's Arms Tavern, St. Paul's Churchyard.

1761.—Sep. 21. Resolved that the Company do make use on the Lord Mayor's Day of their own Linnen, Pewter, Knives, Forks and Glasses.

Resolved that this year no lads who shall attend with their Masters Gowns be permitted to Breakfast at this house but instead thereof they receive one shilling each of the Beadle on their leaving their respective Masters Gowns with him.

1763.—Ap. 25. That the sum of Five Guineas but no more be allowed out of the Cash of the Company to be expended on each of the Quarterly Court Days and if the Bills on those days amount to more that the surplus be raised by the persons present at the said dinner.

1763.—Dec. 8. Admitted Dorothy Gulliver daughter of Thomas Citizen and Turner of London by trade a working Glazier.

1764.—Nov. 4. That no more than One Guinea be allowed out of the Cash of this Company for the Expences of a Private Court Day & that the Surplus of any such Expence be paid by the Members present.

1766.—Sunday, Sep. 21. The Master and Wardens neither attending this meeting at [blank] dissolved in Courte.

1767.—May 21. Furnival Inn Coffee House [Meeting held].

1767.—June 29. The Master acquainted the Court that Mr. John Smith Printseller in Cheapside had made the Company a present of a new Frame to the Picture of the Company's Arms and had also added over the Picture a Shield with an Inscription expressing the time when this Company was incorporated and when invested with a Livery.

1768.—Nov. 9. Mr. Richard Hoar acquainted the Court that Mr. Lake Young late Master of this Company had made the Company a present of a very ellegant Chair for the Master of the Company for the time being to sit in with the Arms of the Company carved and affixed on the Top of the Back.

1768.—Nov. 30. [An estimate for £4. 14. 0 from a carpenter to repair the stand & of an annual fee of Seven Guineas to set it up in St. Pauls Churchyard or any other place appointed once a year, keeping it in good repair meanwhile, was accepted. The stand appears to have had a back of one inch deal panelling with circular ribs overhead, doubtless to support an awning.]

1769.—Nov. 30. Resolved that Six Guineas & no more be allowed out of the Cash of the Company for the expense of a Quarterly Court Dinner.

1770.—April 25. [William Hills, Glassmaker, Shadwell ; the first mention in Minute Books of a Glass *maker*.]

1770.—June 29. Resolved that in future all Quarterly Court Dinners be from this Day for Twenty Persons at 3 Shillings per head & that the Beadle be allowed 2/6 each quarterly Court in lieu of the Dinner.

At this Court Mr. Wm. Cook of Clerkenwell attended & proposed to take the Estate of the Company near Holywell Mount last on lease to Cap^n· Harris for 61 years from Midsummer last at the yearly rent of five guineas clear of Taxes & to build 2 Houses and lay out the sum of £250 on the premises.

1770.—[William Pontifex elected Beadle by Ballot in place of Peter Skelkorn, deceased.]

1771.—Sep. 21. [It was resolved to prosecute all persons carrying on the trade of a Glazier & not having legal right to do so.]

1771.—Oct. 10.   Resolved that if Mr. Bates will take the Pewter of this Company at
9*d.* per pound that it be sold at that price to him.

Resolved that the Linnen and Brass Candlesticks belonging to this Company be sold.

1771.—Nov. 30.   Resolved that it be taken into consideration at the next Court
whether the Company shall go in Procession on the Lord Mayor's Day next.   [It
was resolved on Jan. 25, 1772, not to go in " Processession " because of the expense
and charge.]

1773.—Sep. 30.   Resolved that this Company go in Procession on the next Lord Mayor's
Day.   [The Master & Wardens had seen the Lord Mayor respecting this.   The
" Musick " was to be provided for Six Guineas.]

1774.—Feb. 14.   [By an Order of the House of Commons the Books, Charters, etc., of
the Company were examined by reason of a petition of Mr. John Roberts who complained of an undue Election and Return for the City of London.]

1774.—Ap. 25.   Ordered that the Poor relieved by this Company attend on every
Court Day.

1774.—Oct. 7.   Resolved that a new Livery Gown be provided at the price of £6. 6. 0.

1775.—Oct. 5.   Resolved that it be recommended to the Master and Wardens to cause
sliding Pannels to the Front of the Stand to prevent Persons getting under the Cloth
into the Stand.

1778.—Jan. 26.   Resolved that no Tea or Coffee be had at the Expence of the Company.
Resolved that the Beadle be allowed Ten Shillings and Six Pence in lieu of the
Perquisite of the Victuals remaining of the Dinner.

Resolved that taking into consideration the State of the Finances of the Company
that the Company do not go in Procession on the next Lord Mayor's Day.

1779.—Jan. 25.   Mr. Oliver's Gift for one year 1777 being £3 was paid by the Tenant of
the House in Queen Street Cheapside on which it is chargeable.

1779.—June 10.   [Baptist Head Coffee House, Aldermanbury, a meeting held.]

Minute Book 1779 to 1815.

Principal Meetings at the Queen's Arms Tavern, St. Paul's Churchyard.

Minor Meetings at the Baptist's Head Coffee House.

1780.—June 1.   [A Committee was appointed to view the Company's property in
Queen Street consisting of :—

1. A House at the Corner of Thames Street, let at the time to a Peruke Maker,
    let at £25.

2. The two houses adjoining in Queen Street, let to a Smith, let at £40.

3. The North house adjoining it, let at £27.   A long report is given from a Mr.
    Delight, Surveyor.   The Committee recommended letting the houses on
    repairing leases if possible, as no money was forthcoming from the Company
    apparently for putting the property in repair.]

1780.—June 29.   Resolved that the Annual Dinner of this Company on 29 June be in future in the Country.

1780.—Nov. 30.   Resolved that in future not any suppers be allowed on any Quarterly Court Days at the expense of the Company.

1782.—Ap. 25.   Resolved that the Court dine together on the 29th June next at Cannonbury House, Islington.   [Canonbury House was advertised in 1780 as a suitable resort for invalids on account of the purity of the air and the convenience of a sixpenny stage coach running to the City every hour.]

1782.—Nov. 30.   Resolved that £100 South Sea Annuities be purchased in addition to the Stock now standing in the name of the Company.

1783.—Ap. 25.   Resolved that this Court dine at the Grove House, Camberwell on the next Court Day.   [The Grove House Tea Gardens were largely patronised by certain classes of the metropolis, and the dancing parties at Camberwell Hall were famous.   They were not, strictly speaking, fashionable.   In "Sketches by Boz" is an amusing account of a ball held there by certain aspiring local residents.]
Resolved, that the Stand of the Company be sold.

1783.—Sep. 1.   Resolved that, taking into consideration the state of the finances of the Company that the Company do not go on the Lord Mayor's Day next.

1784.—Jan. 27.   Ordered that the opinion of Counsel be taken how far persons not of the Glazing Business have a right to employ glaziers to work for them and charge for the work when done.

1784.—Oct. 15.   Resolved that the Company do not dine together on Lord Mayor's Day next.

1785.—Jan. 25.   At a Quarterly Court held at the Half Moon Tavern in Cheapside, the Court adjourned to the London Coffee House, Ludgate Hill.

1785.—Ap. 25.   Resolved that £100 Stock be sold out of the Company Stock to defray the Orphans Duty & other demands on this Company.

1786.—Jan. 25.   Ordered that Five Hundred Copies of the By Laws be printed.   [This stock of Bye-Laws has apparently lasted until the present time, 1918, since the Clerk to the Company habitually has one for his general use.]

1786.—Nov. 30.   Resolved that in future there be not any wine or other Refreshment introduced into the Court Room before Dinner.

1791.—Ap. 25.   Resolved that this Company dine on the next Court Day at Mr. Mulletts the Bowling Green House behind the Foundling Hospital.

1792.—Mch. 8.   Resolved that the Company dine at the next Court at the White Hart at Tottenham.

1793.—Jan. 25.   That every Person (excepting the Master and Wardens) introducing a Friend to dine at any Quarterly Court after this Day shall pay for such friend Five Shillings towards the Dinner.
That Dinner be provided on each Quarterly Day for Twenty Persons at Three shillings and Sixpence per head.

1793.—Sep. 21. Ordered that not any Person be admitted into the Freedom of this Company by Redemption in the intervals of the Quarterly Courts but only by Servitude or Patrimony or under the Act of Common Council. That all Persons carrying on the trade of a Glazier or Painter on Glass and not before Free of the City shall be admitted into the Freedom in the Company of Glaziers.

1795.—Ap. 25. Resolved that in consequence of the High Price of Provisions the Dinner on the next Quarterly Court Day be omitted and that each Member attending the Court receive five shillings for his attendance.

1798.—Sep. 21. Resolved that every member of the Company introducing a Friend pay ½ guinea and that the same be specified in the summons.

1798.—Dec. 3. THAT considering the large sum of money which the Renter Warden is already in advance on the Company's Account It is expedient that some mode be adopted to relieve the Finances of the Company.

THAT for this purpose the said committee be empowered to dispose of the Plate belong^s to the Company in such manner as they shall think most advantageous.

THAT the Court do not dine together during the present year on any other days than St. Matthew's Day and St. Andrew's Day and that on these days nothing be allowed at the Company's Expense before Dinner & that the Bill be called at 8 o'clock in the evening precisely.

THAT the Livery Dinner on Lord Mayor's Day be dispensed with.

THAT in future persons desirous of taking on the Livery of the Company be permitted to do, without being obliged first to pay their Steward's fines.

THAT the several fees payable to the Company for the future be as follows :—

	Binding.		s. d.	Freedom.
Company	11. 0			1. 11. 6
Clerk & Indentures ..	1. 9. 6	out of Court	3. 0 ..	3. 6
Beadle	1. 6	do.	1. 0 ..	1. 0
	£2. 2. 0			£1. 16. 0
	Turnover.		Livery.	Assistant.
Company	5. 0 ..		£8. 0. 0 ..	£6. 6. 0
Clerk ..	2. 0 ..		5. 0 ..	7. 6
Beadle	1. 0 ..		2. 6 ..	2. 6
	8. 0		£8. 7. 6	£6. 16. 0

1799.—Ap. 25. The Court proceeded to sell the Plate in several lots to the best Bidders among themselves by the Ounce to be weighed by a proper Person. Several Lots were accordingly purchased by the Members present and the rest was valued by a proper Person appointed by the Committee & taken by him at that Valuation.

Resolved that the Renter Warden do return [Income Tax Return] that the Income of this Company doth not amount to £60 per annum.

Resolved that the Renter Warden to pay 10/6 for the Armorial Bearings Tax for the Company.

Resolved that the Company do not redeem the Land Tax payable out of their estate.

1814.—Ap. 25. Mr. Willis stated that the Court was under great embarrassment for want of a full attendance of the Members. Resolved
THAT from the 30 Nov. last the Court do receive 5/- instead of 2/6 each and that the Fines for non-attendance be 2/6.

1815.—Jan. 25. The Clerk laid before the Court a Copy of an Order of Common Council of 9 May 1671 directing that all persons using the Trade of a Glaziers should be admitted only of this Company.
Resolved that a Caveat be entered in the Chamberlain's Office against the admission of any Persons contrary to the above Order.

Minute Book Jan. 25, 1816 *to Jan.* 25, 1859.

The Meetings were held at the London Coffee House.

1818.—Nov. 30. A list of Prices for Glass, Leading, &c. was submitted and approved. [It is comprehensive, runs into three folios, and is reproduced in this book.]

1820.—[The Commissioners for enquiring into Charities requested that a statement of those in the Glaziers' Company should be forwarded; a long account occurs in the Minute Book giving the reply sent.]

1821.—May 16. [Particulars of repairs, etc., in Nos. 11, 12, Crown Court are given, and further particulars April 25, 1822.]

1822.—Nov. 30. [A long account of the Charities occurs.]

1826.—Jan. 25. A letter from Mr. White was read presenting to the Court a new Chair for the Master.

1828.—Ap. 24. Resolved that the Court do dine in June next at the Plough at Blackwall.

1831.—Jan. 25. Wonderful Chertsey attended and paid his Fine and Fees and was admitted to the Livery.

1832.—Nov. 9. Resolved unanimously that in Future the Father of the Company be excused from Quarterage, Fines and all other payments whatever.

1833.—Sep. 21. Resolved that the payment to the Assistants for their Attendance at the Courts be discontinued until Further Order.

1836.—Ap. 11. That the Thanks of the Court be given to Mr. Fenton for newly embellishing the Company's Arms.

1844.—Ap. 25. Resolved unanimously That Mr. Wm. Houlder be removed from the Court of Assistants on the ground of Misbehaviour. List of Books, Papers, and Deeds handed to Mr. Chas. Henry Lovell on his taking the office of Clerk.

1845.—Ap. 7. A list of Prices of Glass, Work, &c. printed was presented to this Court, and a copy of the same is pasted in the Minute Book.

1845.—Sep. 22. Ordered that a Dinner be provided on Lord Mayor's Day free of expense for such of the Livery as have paid their Steward's Fine and Quarterage and for the Livery admitted within the last three years.

PRICES OF GLAZIER'S WORK,

ALLOWED BY THE

MASTER, WARDENS, AND COURT OF ASSISTANTS,

OF THE

WORSHIPFUL COMPANY OF GLAZIERS,

LONDON.

NOVEMBER 30, 1818.

CROWN GLASS IN NEW SASHES.	Best.	Seconds.	Thirds.
Squares of 3 Feet ....per Foot	4s.	3s. 6d.	3s.
Ditto ... 2 Feet 6 Inches .... ditto	3s. 6d.	3s. 2d.	2s. 8d.
Ditto ... 2 Feet .... ditto	3s. 2d.	2s. 8d.	2s. 3d.
Ditto ... Under 2 Feet .... ditto	3s.	2s. 6d.	2s.

GROUND GLASS.

In Squares of 3 Feet .... per Foot 5s. 6d. | In Squares of 2 Feet 6 ...... per Foot 5s. 0d.
In Squares of 2 Feet .... per Foot 4s. 6d.

BENT GLASS IN NEW SASHES.

Three Feet to 3 Feet 3 ...... per Foot 7s. 0d. | Two Feet 6 to 2 Feet .... per Foot 5s. 6d.
Three Feet to 2 Feet 6 ...... ditto 6s. 0d. | Under 2 Feet .... ditto 5s. 0d.
Old Work 6d. per Foot extra.

GREEN GLASS.

In New Sashes .... per Foot 1s. 6d. | Old Glass at the Risk of the Employer per Foot 8d.

NEWCASTLE CROWN GLASS STOPPED IN OLD SASHES.

Squares of 3 Feet .... per Foot 4s. 4d. | Squares of 2 Feet.......... per Foot 3s. 4d.
Ditto 2 Feet 6 .... ditto 3s. 10d. | Ditto under 2 Feet........ ditto 3s. 0d.

Ground Glass stopped in old Sashes per Ft. 5s. 6d. | Green Glass stopped in old Sashes per Ft. 2s. 0d.

LEAD LIGHTS, CROWN OR GREEN GLASS.

In Quarries or Squares 6 by 4 . per Foot 1s. 8d. | In Sqrs. above 6 by 4 and under 8 by 6 ditto 1s. 10d.
In Squares 8 by 6 to 10 by 8 per Foot 2s. 0d.

QUARRIES AND SQUARES STOPPED IN OLD LIGHTS.

Quarries .... each 0s. 4d. | Squares above 7 by 5 to 8 by 6 ... ditto 0s. 8d.
Squares under 7 by 5 .... ditto 0s. 5d. | Ditto .... 8 by 6 to 9 by 7 ... each 1s. 0d.
Ditto above 9 by 7 to 10 by 8 ... each 1s. 3d.

New Leading Old Lights.... per Foot 0s. 10d. | Puttying Windows or Sky-lights one Side
Repairing . . ditto .... ditto 0s. 6d. | only .... per Dozen Squares 0s. 8d.
Cementing Lights............. ditto 0s. 3d. | Cleaning Windows, common Size .. each 0s. 6d.
Casements Pinned in .... each 6d. to 1s. | Ditto, Venetians, common Size .... ditto 1s. 0d.
Puttying Windows or Sky-lights both Sides} ..... 1s. 0d. | Ditto, Lead Lights, ditto .... ditto 0s. 2d.
per Dozen Squares................

Plate Glass, Large Flat Crown Glass, and Moulded Glass, to be specially agreed for according to the Sizes.

Work done in Churches, Public Buildings, &c. to be valued according to the Labour
and difficulty in executing the same.

Signed by Order of the Court,

J. HINDMAN, *Clerk.*

[*Price One Shilling & Sixpence.*]

Printed by W. M'Dowall, Pemberton Row, Gough Square.

1845.—Dec. 1. An Inventory of the Articles delivered to the Renter Warden :—

A Livery Gown	The Beadle's Gown
A Green Baize Table Cover	Five Banners
The Beadle's Staff	Charter, Morocco Bound
2 Scrolls with Wax Seals	6 old Books
A Bell	A Hammer
Copper Plate of Invitation Card	Box with Accounts & Books

Chest with old papers & drawer with Company's Arms.

1846.—Ap. 25. Ordered that a Dinner be provided for the Court at the West India Dock Tavern, Blackwall, on June 29.

1847.—Ap. 27. Ordered that a Dinner be provided for the Court at the Brunswick Hotel, Blackwall, on June 29th next.

1848.—Nov. 30. [A letter was received from the Comptroller's Office, Guildhall, stating that the Corporation of London desired to purchase No. 61 Queen Street for City improvement.]

1849.—Feb. 8. [The Surveyor's Report upon the premises was read, and is very comprehensive ; he valued the house at £3,842. Ordered that the Clerk send in a claim for £4,500.]

1849.—Sep. 21. [The Sub-Committee reported that £4,000 had been mutually agreed upon between themselves & the Corporation for 61 Queen Street. The Court agreed to the sale on those terms.]

1850.—Ap. 25. [The Clerk reported that the £4,000 had been invested in the purchase of £4,183. 0. 2 Reduced Annuities.]

1850.—Ap. 21. Resolved that the payment of 5/- to the members of the Court for their attendance be resumed as heretofore.

1853.—Ap. 25. Ordered that the Company invest the South Sea Annuities with £2. 10. 0 p.c. Stock with addition of £10 to the Capital.

1856.—Ap. 25. Ordered that the Seal of the Company be affixed to a Petition praying that the Bill for amending the Corporation of the City of London may not pass.

Extracts from Minute Book, 1859 to 1888 and 1888 to 1918.

The most prominent features in the Minutes for this period are those referring to investments of the Company's money, the capital being transferred from one security to another according to the inducements offered. There are also a considerable number of letters of condolence entered in full, relating to departed members of the Livery. The different places of meeting and holding the Courts were the London Coffee House, in St. Paul's Churchyard, to 29th June, 1867 ; Radley's Hotel, in New Bridge Street, to 29th June,

1871 ; and the Guildhall Coffee House for the few times after that date, until the Cannon Street Hotel could be obtained, the first meeting in which was on September 21st, 1871 ; it remained the headquarters of the Company until 1918, when the use of the Painter Stainers' Hall was secured, the first court there being on the 21st day of January, 1918.

The years from 1880 to 1885-6 were very anxious times for the City Companies. A Royal Commission was appointed in 1880 to enquire into the finances, objects and mode of government of the Companies ; it was brought about by a Parliamentary section of extreme Liberal tendencies, who were bent upon a so-called re-organisation of the Fraternities which, if sanctioned, would inevitably have resulted in their virtual extinction. Happily the storm was successfully weathered, and the Commission proved a blessing in disguise by serving to strengthen and shield the ancient organisations against extremists in future times of stress. In 1884, at the critical phase of the struggle, a new Clerk was appointed by the Glaziers' Company in the person of Mr. James Berriman Tippetts, and, either from the stimulating effects of the crisis, or by this infusion of fresh blood, or from both causes, certain it is that the Fraternity entered upon a new lease of life and exhibited a rejuvenescence which was in marked contrast to the previous two decades. The brethren appear to have lapsed during that period into a semi-moribund condition, and it is difficult to discover from the Minute Book any evidence of progress ; the year 1884, when the new Clerk was appointed, is the turning point, and the Minutes, which formerly occupied a half-page or less, now run into one or two folios for each Meeting, while such innovations as the Company inviting the Sheriffs to dinner, entertaining the Lord Mayor, providing suitable regalia and jewellery, and taking an effective interest in City life and progress, are evidences of a stimulated life in marked contrast with the preceding placid existence. Naturally the reaction was expensive, since the proverbial omelette entails the sacrifice of eggs, but the Company was satisfied with the progress made and cheerfully went without their dinner in 1887 as a necessary retrenchment. One result of the energy and enterprise exhibited was the increase of the Livery from 27 in 1875 to 64 in 1896 ; and now in January, 1919, 110 in number ; the Assistants also increased from 10 in the first year mentioned, to 16 in 1890, and are now, 1919, 16 in number.

In the Minute Book, 1888 to 1919, we find a continuation of the vigorous policy initiated in the previous years, and a steady period of solid prosperity ensuing. The fines were increased in order to add to the revenue, the regalia was augmented by the munificence of individual members, while the Livery remained satisfactory in numbers thus maintaining the substantial additions it had witnessed in 1896.

Minute Book, 1859 to 1888.

25 April, 1862.—A well-worded Address of Condolence to the Queen upon the demise of the Prince Consort is given in full.

30 June, 1864.—A Dinner was held at the Brunswick Hotel, Blackwall.

23 March, 1867.—Resolved that the £4,183. 0. 2. Reduced Annuities and £400 part of the £850 2½ p.c. Annuities be sold out and the proceeds invested in the purchase of £4,000 City Debenture Bonds, part of the loan for the Holborn Valley improvement bearing interest at £4. 15. 0. per cent.

26 April, 1869.—A Motion that each Member of the Court have the privilege of introducing a Lady at the annual dinner was negatived.

25 April, 1870.—Resolved that on and after this day the payment to the Assistants attending each Court be 10/-.

21 Sept., 1870.—The Clerk reported that some of the Books and property of the Company had been damaged by an overflow of Sewage into the basement of Radley's Hotel and that Messrs. Fuller had been instructed to negotiate for compensation.

Resolved that an Inventory be made of the Company's property for the use of the Renter Warden.

18 Aug., 1871.—A Meeting was held in the Guildhall Coffee House.

21 Sept., 1871.—First Meeting at Cannon Street Hotel.

29 June, 1872.—A Dinner held at the Ship Hotel, Greenwich.

30 June, 1873.—A Dinner held at the Crystal Palace.

26 Jan., 1874.—The City Chamberlain announced that the City Bonds would be repaid, or renewed at 4 p.c.

Resolved to offer a renewal at the present rate.

25 April, 1874.—The Clerk announced that the City had refused to renew the bonds and the £4,000 was therefore ordered to be invested in New Zealand Bonds.

29 June, 1874.—Resolved that no Quarterage or Fines should in future be collected from the Court.

30 Nov., 1874.—Thomas Lovell was appointed to discharge the duties of Beadle temporarily during the pleasure of the Court.

21 Sept., 1875.—The Master produced to the Court a Jewel appropriate for the Master of the Company, the price of which he stated to be £14. 14. 0. Resolved that it should be purchased, and at the request of the Court the Master decorated himself with the jewel.

9 Nov., 1875.—Thomas Lovell elected Beadle.

29 June, 1876.—A Dinner was held at the Alexandra Palace.

29 June, 1881.—A Dinner was held at the Star and Garter Hotel, Richmond.

30 Nov., 1881.—It was reported to the Court that inventories had been made of the papers and property of the Company and that a tin box had been ordered for the Charters, Deeds and Documents and deposited at the Bank of England.

25 Jan., 1882.—A full list of Charters, Deeds, Documents, etc., given at this Court.

30 Nov., 1882.—Resolved that the Master's Old Arm Chair be presented to Mr. F. W. Jones at his request.

25 April, 1884.—A Dinner for the Court was ordered to be provided for June 30 at Hampton Court or Richmond.

2 Oct., 1884.—Mr. James Berriman Tippetts was unanimously elected Clerk to the Company in the place of Mr. C. H. Lovell, and on October 7 is given the list of Books, Deeds, etc., handed over to his keeping.

25 April, 1885.—The Meeting was occupied chiefly with the consideration of the " Bill for the better securing their property to Corporate or quasi-Corporate Associations."

15 July, 1885.—£500 to be invested in New 3 p.c. Government Stock.

9 Nov., 1885.—Resolved that the Sheriffs of London and their Under Sheriffs be invited as Guests of the Company to the dinner to be held on the 30 Nov. instant.

28 April, 1886.—Court and a Dinner held at the Mitre Hotel, Hampton Court. The question of presenting to each of the Past Masters a medal of the Badge of Office was considered, and

25 May, 1886.—On this date the Badge was approved and ordered to be executed in Gold and Enamel, the cost not to exceed five guineas.

21 Sept., 1886.—The Past Masters to the number of six were presented with Badges. The Lord Mayor was reported to have accepted the invitation of the Company to Dinner.

9 Nov., 1886.—Resolved that Badges be used by the Upper and Renter Wardens.

30 Nov., 1886.—A robe was purchased for the use of the Clerk.

21 Sept., 1887.—Resolved that no dinner be held after the Court Meeting of 25 Jan.

21 Sept., 1888.—Resolved to purchase for £1,100 ground rents in Woolf Street and to sell New Zealand Bonds for that purpose.

Minute Book, 25 Jan., 1889, to present year.

25 April, 1889.—The Clerk requested the Court to accept from him a Photographic Album to hold photographs of the Masters of the Company.

The thanks of the Court were accorded him and a suitable box to hold the album was ordered.

30 Jan., 1891.—Resolved that the Lord Mayor and Sheriffs be invited to dine with the Court of this Company on April 25.

27 April, 1891.—The Master (Mr. Frank Green) was congratulated upon his appointment as Alderman of the City of London, and in returning thanks requested the Company to accept a Banner bearing his Coat of Arms to be placed with other Banners and Pennons of the Company.

28 June, 1892.—The Clerk's Report upon the Financial condition of the Company showed that the shifting of an uncertain amount of Income had appreciably increased during the 10 years past, and that a former income from corporate property had become considerably lessened.

21 Sept., 1892.—The Report of the Special Committee appointed to investigate the Financial affairs of the Company is put down in full under this date, and the Clerk's Report occurs on page 82.

25 April, 1893.—The Recommendations of the Special Committee were considered and the new Fines and Fees were considered and duly passed.

29 June, 1893.—The questions addressed to the Clerk by Members *re* Fines, etc., are replied to here.

9 Nov., 1895.—The Master expressed a wish for Ladies to be present at the Banquet to be held on the 30th inst. and offered to defray all expenses connected with this invitation. The Court agreed to the proposal.

25 Jan., 1896.—Votes of thanks were accorded to the Master and Mr. Thorne for the great pleasure afforded at the late Banquet by the presence of ladies.

25 Jan., 1897.—A Report was given in respecting the financial status of the Company.

21 Sept., 1898.—The Court was informed of the death of their late Clerk, Mr. W. J. B. Tippetts, and unanimously passed a vote of condolence. His son, Mr. W. J. B. Tippetts, was appointed Clerk.

30 Nov., 1900.—The Master, Benjamin Scott F. McGeogh, presented to the Company a Master's Jewel to be held by the Company in perpetuity. Resolved that the Master's jewel be attached by a blue ribbon and all other jewels by red.

9 Nov., 1901.—The Court ordered that a letter of congratulation be sent to Sir Frank Green, Bart., Past Master of the Company, upon the honour conferred upon him by the King. Mr. F. E. Spicer, a Liveryman of the Company, presented to the Company a Silver Loving Cup.

STAINED GLASS WINDOW SHOWING ARMS OF THE COMPANY OF
GLAZIERS AND PAINTERS OF GLASS IN THE NEW TOWN HALL,
DERRY, IRELAND, AFTER THE GREAT DERRY FIRE, AND WHEN
PAST MASTER W. J. B. TIPPETTS, C.C., WAS DEPUTY-GOVERNOR
OF THE IRISH SOCIETY OF THE CITY OF LONDON.

27 May, 1902.—It was resolved that the privilege of inviting one lady (to the Court Dinner) at the expense of the Company be given to each member of the Court in addition to the ordinary privileges.

21 July, 1902.—It was resolved to present a Silver Spoon, engraved with the Arms of the Company, to each lady guest on the occasion of their attending the Summer Dinner.

23 Sept., 1902.—Resolved that one-half of the net amount of all fees received be invested and added to the other investments of the Company.

25 April, 1905.—It was arranged that the Summer Dinner be held at Nuthall's, Kingston-on-Thames.

25 April, 1906.—Resolved that the Summer Dinner be held at the Mitre, Hampton Court.

30 Nov., 1908.—Mr. Dyke stated that he had consulted a friend of his, Mr. Ernest C. Collings, Heraldic Painter, in reference to the Arms of the Company, and had obtained from him a properly coloured sketch and description of the Arms, which he handed to the Company, and it was decided that the same should be entered in the Minute Book. [The coloured sketch is duly entered, together with the description as quoted in Chap. VI.]

26 April, 1909.—Mr. W. R. Skinner was temporarily appointed Beadle in place of Mr. Thomas Lovell, deceased ; this was confirmed at the next Court.

30 Nov., 1909.—A letter from Mr. Walter J. De Pearce is given containing information respecting the teaching and encouragement of the Art of Stained Glass Window making and of Leaded Lights, which had been asked for by Mr. N. Kilvert. A Committee was appointed to report upon the letter.

23 Sept., 1910.—Mr. Dyas reported upon his investigations respecting the presentation of Prizes to encourage Glaziers' work, and it was resolved to let the matter remain in abeyance.

9 Nov., 1910.—An autograph Book for members was presented to the Company by the Renter Warden, Mr. Henry Edmunds.

25 Jan., 1911.—Resolved that the Company should, according to its means, contribute to the proposed Memorial Windows in the New Town Hall in Derry, and the Master supplemented the amount to be given by his own subscription of five guineas.

25 Jan., 1912.—The Master, Mr. Henry Edmunds, presented to the Company a Silver Bowl and Ladle of American workmanship.

20 Sept., 1912.—The Clerk, Mr. W. J. B. Tippetts, resigned his post and his son, Mr. Percy W. B. Tippetts, was nominated in his place.

9 Nov., 1912.—Confirmation of election of the Clerk, Mr. Percy W. B. Tippetts.

21 Sept., 1914.—The Pensioners were paid on this occasion for the first time in the One Pound Notes which had been issued by the Government to relieve the financial strain which was anticipated in consequence of the war with Germany.

The Lord Mayor's Day Banquet was postponed in consequence of the War and a cheque for 25 guineas was given to the Red Cross Fund.

30 Nov., 1914.—Resolved that a donation of 25 guineas be given to the *Daily Telegraph* Belgian Relief Fund, and 25 guineas also to Mr. G. Paget Walford, Renter Warden, for distribution among the various Belgian Relief Funds in which he was interested.

26 April, 1915.—The Clerk made a Report regarding the Trusts of the Company, and it was resolved that in future the Trust income should be wholly expended, in grants to pensioners and otherwise, in the year when it accrued.

1 May, 1916.—Resolved that the Stocks held by the Company be converted into Exchequer Bonds and War Loan.

1 July, 1916.—The Master reported that he had visited the Senior Pensioner, Mr. David Leslie, who was the oldest member of the Livery of the Company, having been admitted in 1839, and would attain the age of 100 years on Jan. 17th, 1917.

21 Sept., 1916.—The Master, Mr. W. J. B. Tippetts, thanked the Court for the handsome presents given by the Company on the occasion of his recent marriage.

9 Nov., 1916.—Resolved that £5 be sent to the *Daily Telegraph* Christmas Puddings Fund, and £5 to the National Committee for Relief in Belgium. [In this latter fund Master G. Paget Walford took a great and keen interest, having lived many years in Antwerp.]

30 Nov., 1916.—Resolved that in view of the exceptional circumstances prevailing by reason of the great European war, the sum of £2 be given to each of the Pensioners at Christmas. At the same Court it was ordered that Mr. David Leslie be presented with 100 crowns, with the congratulations of the Company and a suitable framed address.

25 Jan., 1917.—Resolved that £2,100 5 per cent. Exchequer Bonds held by the Company be converted into 5 per cent. War Loan Stock.

25 April, 1917.—The Master (Mr. Geo. Paget Walford) reported with regret the deaths of three Past Masters, viz.: Geo. Thistle Thornes, Stephen Woodbridge, and Matthew Wallace.

Among those admitted to the Freedom were Charles Frederick Fenton, whose ancestors had been members of the Company since, at the least, the 10th May, 1750.

21 Sept., 1917.—Mr. Harry Seymour Foster, the Upper Warden, reported fully upon the Representation of the People Bill, 1917, as to the Clause affecting the Livery Companies, and a grant of ten guineas was made towards a fund formulated to oppose certain parts of the Bill.

A donation of £7 10s. was made to the Y.M.C.A. Hut at Camberwell, for entertaining the Wounded Soldiers to tea.

The Master congratulated Mr. Past Master Proctor on that day being the fiftieth anniversary of his being sworn as a Liveryman of the Company.

9 Nov., 1917.—It was resolved to call the Livery together at an early date to explain the effect of the Bill before Parliament upon their ancient rights.

The Master announced that he would invite the Livery to dine with him as his guests, to commemorate his election for the third time in succession as Master, the history of the Company since 1328 showing no such record.

29 Nov., 1917.—The Court was held at Girdlers' Hall. It was resolved that in view of the exceptional circumstances occasioned by the War the sum of two pounds should be sent to each of the Pensioners at Christmas. To the Senior Pensioner, Mr. David Leslie, it was resolved that one hundred and one new shillings should be presented on the occasion of his 101st birthday, 17 January, 1918.

21 Jan., 1918.—The Court was held at Painters' Hall, and seven new Liverymen were sworn in.

The Master outlined his scheme for raising a Special Fund to encourage the glass-making and glass-painting industry.

Letters were read supporting the suggested use of Painters' Hall for the Meetings of the Glaziers' Company.

28 Jan., 1918.—It was reported that the Senior Liveryman and Pensioner, Mr. David Leslie, had died suddenly on the 26th inst., aged 101. The proposed Technical Education Scheme was further discussed, and a letter from the Master was read contributing 200 guineas towards the Fund as a nucleus.

Dr. Bradley reported fully as to the "Society of Glass Technology" at the University of Sheffield. It was resolved that the Company become a Member of the Society. The Clerk was instructed to invest £600 in 4 per cent. National War Bonds when the Tank Visit occurred.

25 April, 1918.—At this Court Mr. Dudley Forsyth was appointed Instructor of the Classes at the Trades Training School.

The Clerk reported twelve candidates for the Livery, and it was resolved that the next Court be held at Hampton Court on 29 June.

A vote of thanks was accorded to Mr. Harry Seymour Foster, and congratulations upon his success with regard to the Representation of the People Act, 1918, and it was resolved that an illuminated testimonial be presented to him to mark the appreciation of the Company.

13 June, 1918.—The congratulations of the Court were tendered to Sir Harry Seymour Foster upon the Knighthood recently conferred upon him.

A donation of £21 was made towards the Lord Mayor's Silver Wedding Fund to commemorate the 25th anniversary of the marriage of the King and Queen, and 15 guineas to the British Red Cross Society and Order of St. John of Jerusalem.

The Master presented two handsome silver loving cups to the Company as a mark of his appreciation of the honour conferred upon him by the Company in electing him to the Mastership for the third time.

30 July, 1918.—The Master reported fully upon the Technical Education Scheme of the Company, and it was resolved that the Fund raised should be devoted solely to the encouragement of the Scheme.

The Clerk was instructed to purchase £500 4 per cent. National War Bonds, 1927.

At the Lunch which followed upon the Meeting of this Court the Lord Mayor of London, the Sheriffs, the Solicitor-General (Sir Gordon Stewart), Sir David Murray, Sir Acton Blake, K.C.M.G., Sir Trevor Dawson, R.N., and other distinguished guests were present.

25 Sept., 1918.—The Master, George Paget Walford, was unanimously re-elected Master for the ensuing year (being the fourth time, and the third in succession) upon the proposal of the Senior Warden, Sir Harry Foster, and the Renter Warden, Mr. Charles Grimwade, as seconder.

The Beadle, Mr. W. R. Skinner, resigned, and Qr.-Master-Sergt. Geo. F. Pittock was elected in his place.

The Master reported upon the progress made with the " History of the Glaziers' Company," and stated that he proposed making the book a gift to the Company and presenting each Member with a copy.

Nine candidates for admission were elected.

At the Luncheon the Members were addressed by Dr. Turner, of the Sheffield University, and other gentlemen interested in Glass manufacture.

Extracts from Minute Book to present time.

We have now traced the Worshipful Company of Glaziers and Painters of Glass through some seven or more centuries, from the time when their Guild first came into being, caused by the erstwhile luxury of glass becoming a necessity of civilised existence, to the present time. It now occupies an honoured place among the skilled arts and crafts of our national life, while the stained-glass window with gilded leads is within the reach of all that are aesthetically inclined. But while the Art of the Mystery has thus satisfactorily evolved during the lapse of passing centuries, we must not lose sight of the fact that the social amenities also have progressed, and, although in the main the same as of yore, have assumed the polish of progress and the touch of the times.

The more ancient of our Glaziers derived their amusement, recreation and relaxation after work almost entirely from the Church, which provided not only spiritual encouragement and food for the mind, but was also the Theatre of the time, the Church and Stage then being one. At Oberammagau we have a survival of those Mystery Plays which the artizan with his wife and family flocked to witness at the local Church ; while in the troubadour, tymbestere, jongleur and itinerant story-teller we have practically all the concomitants of the modern Music Hall. The social club was represented at that time by the ale-house with its inviting bush displayed outside ; not by any means similar to its modern prototype, but a universal shelter where a good plain meal, simple, honest, home-brewed ale, a good fire, and homely, hearty company cheered the toiler after a day's work.

Later on, when the stage and its connections became so debased that even Elizabethan London, none too particular in its distinctions, relegated the Theatres to Bank Side and would not tolerate them within the City Walls, the Glazier of the time took to sport, such as coursing and hunting, together with the dubious recreations of cock-fighting and bull-baiting, while the Guild feasts assumed a greater importance in his life than hitherto as a means of temporarily throwing off the cares of life. The call of the countryside evoked a responsive echo in his bosom, and we find him revelling in the delights of Somers Town, of Kentish Green and Paddington, not to mention the rural charms of remote spots like Blackheath and Hampstead.

In the Georgian Period eating and drinking became fine arts, and if our Glazier succumbed to their allurements we must blame human nature and its gregarious instincts which prompt imitation of the bad as well as the good. We can hardly imagine a self-respecting Glazier in the " March to Finchley," or of any of the bacchanalian orgies immortalised by Hogarth, when horse-play was the only method of practical joking, and the hurling of a glass bottle through the window where a harmless citizen sat around the table with wife and children was accounted gentle and joyous humour.

H 2

Lord Mayor's Day was then the hub of the London Freemen's wheel of life, for from it radiated sufficient material for conversation for the ensuing year; the glories of the past pageant and the anticipation of the future assumed paramount importance in his existence. Among the archives of the Glaziers' Company are found many old accounts relating to various items of expenditure and some, especially the bills of fare, are of considerable interest. Here, for example, is an undated sample, but from the writing probably about 1680 or 1700 :—

								s.	d.
Bread and Beer	..	..	..	..	..	..		1	6
Wine ..	..	..	..	..	..	..	..	11	6
Dressing the Dinner with Bacon and greenes				..	..		4	0
Cheese ..	..	..	..	..	..	..	..		2
Tobacco	..	..	..	..	..	..	..		3
Pd for Lamb ..	..	..	..	..	..	..		3	0
Tartts ..	..	..	..	..	..	..	..	2	0
Drawer	..	..	..	..	..	..	..		7
							£1	3	0

The "sevenpence" to the "Drawer" has a Falstaffian atmosphere which is quite refreshing.

One bill at the Baptist Head Coffee House, 1798, is in striking contrast to present prices :—

Sandwiches, rum, milk, chocolate, etc.	..	..	..	4d.
Waiter ..	..	..	..	4d.

Probably present day prices would compare favourably with the following :—

8, St. Paul's Alley, St. Paul's Churchyard.

1798.—To 27 plates Best Fruits, 2/6 .. .. £3. 7. 6.

Early eighteenth century prices may be judged by :—

Oct. 29, 1746—Coffee, ½ lb. ..	..	..	..	..	2. 9.
Sugar, 1 lb. ..		..	..		1. 0.
					3. 9.

The Beadle's Bill (John Wotton) of the same year also furnishes prices, etc. :—

To 10 quartern loaves	4. 4½
1 lb. of Candles	7
Rowles (rolls) cheese and strong beer	9

and the following Dinner Bill (1746) may be given :—

5 dishes of Mince pyes	15. 0.
6 buttered apple pyes	18. 0.
For Fresh Butter, Flower and salt butter for the Range	12. 0.
Sage Horseradish beteroot & savrell	3. 0.
Gravy Onion Sauce and Apple Sauce	4. 0.
Lemons anchoves and spice	4. 0.
Vinegar pepper and salt for ye tables	2. 0.
Dressing Dinner	1. 11. 6.
Use Linnin Knives forkes pewter	3. 0. 0.
Lost 8 Spoons 2 plates	3. 4.

We would willingly omit the last item, but perhaps the plates were of pewter and therefore irresistible.

An Assistants' Dinner of Nov. 30, 1797, is as follows :—

Bread and Beer	7. 0.
Dinners	4. 4. 0.
Cheese and Butter	7. 0.
Strong Beer	7. 6.
Lisbon	10. 6.
Old Port	5. 19. 0.
Sherry	1. 7. 0.
Brandy	3. 6.
Lemons Sugar & Nutmeg	6. 0.
Tobacco and Snuff	4. 6.
Refreshments in the morning	17. 6.
Beadle's Dinner	2. 0.
Broken Glass	1. 0.
	14. 13. 6.
Waiters	10. 6.
	15. 4. 0.

The " Refreshments in the morning " affords food for thought.   In 1801 the numbers of diners on Lord Mayor's Day is given as 83, and the Bill amounted to £65. 15. 8.   One 18th century bill contains the item " for 5 Tanseys, 15/-."   The Tansey was a cake or pudding flavoured with the common tansy and eaten generally at Easter.

As the reader might possibly imagine that the Glaziers' Company was somewhat parsimonious in the matter of its feasts in the olden times, judging from the preceding, a Bill of Fare preserved among the old papers in the Charter box is reproduced here which may possibly dispel the illusion.   The cost of this symposium is not given.

London Coffee House, Lord Mayor's Day, Nov. 9th, 1798.

Dinner for the Master, Wardens, Assistants and Liverymen of the Worshipful Company of Glaziers.

Bill of Fare.

6   Dishes of fine Cod boiled with Fryed Smelts round each Dish with a proper quantity of Oyster and Shrimp Sauce to each dish.

2   Fine Hams boiled weighing about 20 lbs. each.

6   Dishes of fine Fowls 1 boiled and 2 roasted in each dish with a proper quantity of oyster and gravy sauce.

1   surloin of Fine Beef roasted and 1 Buttock of fine Beef boiled each to weigh about 20 lbs. with a proper quantity of Pickles Horse-Radish Greens and Sallad.

6   fine Turkeys roasted with a proper quantity of sausages and Gravy Sauce to each dish.

6   dishes of fine Wild Ducks 2 in each Dish with a proper quantity of Onion and Gravy Sauce to each Dish.

4   plumb puddings.

4   fine Marrow Puddings.

4   dishes of fine Mince Pies 3 in each dish.

6   dishes of fine Lobsters boiled.

6   dishes of fine Fricassees.

4   dozen and 3 quarts of Fine Red Port Wine.

2   dozen and 3 quarts of Fine White Port Wine.

2   gallons of the best Rum and 2 gallons of the best Brandy with a proper quantity of Oranges and Lemons and Sugar to make it into Punch.

1   best Gloucester Cheese weighing about 8 lbs.

With a proper quantity or proportion of Greens, Potatoes Beer Butter Bread Vinegar Oil Pepper Salt Mustard &c.

And a proper number of Knives Forks Plates Dishes Spoons Linen Table Cloths Napkins Mugs and Glasses and suitable Lights for the occasion.

And also Firing Servants Waiters and Attendants proper and proportionable to the said Bill of Fare.

Dinner to be ready at 4 of the Clock in the Afternoon precisely.

The Glazier of the present day, when seated at the festal board, presents the polished and refined replica of the mediaeval and renaissance guildsman. He appreciates the good things of the table fully as much as his progenitor, but limits the amount of food taken to that which produces the maximum quantity of bodily comfort, combined with that indulgence in the flowing bowl which "maketh glad the heart of man" and no more. He is just as fond of a good tale well told, of a suitable song well sung, of the " feast of wisdom and the flow of soul " as in olden times ; he sheds tears of delight at the crisp crackle of a good joke, a clever retort, a quip or crank of merit, or a harmless practical joke. He shares with his colleagues in the rich feeling of satisfaction which benevolence at the previous business meeting invariably engenders, and is the embodied personification of the happy and contented man. In business connected with the Company's affairs he can be as obdurate as his antecedent of the Middle Ages, as is instanced by his defiance of a Royal Commission in 1880 in refusing to send in statements of the Company's affairs which he deemed inquisitive. The whole amount of the income from the Corporate estate of the Company is expended upon good works, and the Glazier's only regret is that he cannot do more.

Upon the fly-leaves of the Minute Books are numerous memoranda, many of an interesting character, jotted down by various persons.   Two are appended :—

(*Minute Book*, 1779 *to* 1815.)

" Mr. Letchley (punch)   Pint of Milk   ⎱ boiled
                             Spoonful of Rosemary ⎰ to ½ pint."
                     Sweetened with Honey.

" Musick 1773

" Mr. Strong ⎱ 2 horns		Coopers' Hall
Mr. Hill ⎰		Sheriff's Office, Wood Street
Mr. Mallet	1st Clarionett	Spittlefields
Mr. Cook	2nd ,,	Piccadilly
Mr. Lusloo	1st Bassoon	belonging to the Guards
Mr. —	2nd ,,	belonging to the Westminster Militia.

CHAPTER XI.

ADVANTAGES OF MEMBERSHIP AND FUTURE SCOPE OF
THE COMPANY.

THE advantages ensuing from the Membership of a London City Company are so many and so complicated that it is practically impossible to enumerate them all in detail with any definiteness or exactitude, as the benefits may directly or indirectly appear in unsuspected situations which are quite beyond the realm of forethought. This condition is brought about by the fact that during five or six centuries it was absolutely necessary in cases of preferment in the City of London that the candidate for the post should be the member of a Company or Guild. Although this necessity no longer prevails the tradition has passed into an unwritten law, almost or quite as rigid as when it appeared on the statutes.

When a name is mentioned as being that of a man who might safely be entrusted with a post, the question "To what Company does he belong?" arises as a matter of course; and should the answer be that "he is of no Company whatever," it is always possible that interest in his application ceases. It is one of those little things that, perhaps, should not be, and is undeniably outside the pale of defence, but all the time that human nature remains as it is so long will the little things prevail, and it behoves everyone who seeks advancement to bear this in mind.

In the month of November the election of the Lord Mayor of London occurs, and only Liverymen are permitted to record votes on that occasion. In June the annual election of the London Sheriffs, two Almoners and two Bridge Masters occurs, and the same regulations prevail.

These privileges lend a dignity to the position of a Liveryman commensurate with the importance accruing from the proper government of a great Capital, and the thoroughness, precision, and exhaustive scrutiny attending elections is a convincing guarantee that the correct men have attained the coveted position.

The Company of Glaziers and Painters of Glass undoubtedly has a future before it which will bear favourable comparison with the position it maintained throughout the mediaeval period and that of the Renaissance. With the increase of the numbers of the Livery, which is very promising and encouraging at the present time, the long projected wishes and aims of the Fraternity will mature to successful fruition. Some of those contemplated movements, which are essentially educational and socially progressive in their inception, may with advantage be included here, and the following, kindly contributed by Sir Harry Foster, Upper Warden of the Company, treats of this subject :—

The Great War which has ravaged the world since August, 1914, has just been brought to a victorious conclusion by the signature of an Armistice with Germany on 11th November last, and the great work of Reconstruction of the World's Industries is about to commence. In anticipation of this work the Government, through Dr. Addison, the Minister for Reconstruction, made an earnest appeal to the Livery Companies of London, in the early part of this year, to re-establish a close connection with the Crafts or Trades with which they were originally identified and which called them into being.

The Company of Glaziers and Painters of Glass were among the first to respond to this appeal, under the guidance and inspiration of Mr. George Paget Walford, who had served the office of Master in 1904, and again in 1916-17 and 1918, and upon whom the Court conferred the unique honour of re-election for the third year in succession in September, 1918, as a special recognition of the Reconstruction work inaugurated on his initiative.

As a first step in this work, and with the fraternal assistance of the Worshipful Company of Carpenters, practical classes for craftsmen in stained glass and other glazing, open to those engaged in the trade, have been inaugurated at the Trades Training Schools of the Carpenters' Company, 153, Great Titchfield Street, which are under the direction of Mr. Sheriff Banister Fletcher, F.R.I.B.A., F.S.I., the instructor being

Mr. Dudley Forsyth, one of the leading artists in stained glass in this country and a Liveryman of the Glaziers' Company. The intention of the Court is that this shall develop, amongst other things :

1. The Registration of—(*a*) Painters of Glass.
   (*b*) Apprentices.
   (*c*) Master Glaziers.

2. Exhibitions of modern Stained-Glass Work and of Leaded Lights, with examples of the Mediaeval and Renaissance periods.

3. Medals and prizes for the best examples of Stained-Glass and Leaded Lights.

4. Diplomas to accredited manufacturers of Stained-Glass and Leaded Lights.

5. Co-operation with the Sheffield University in Lecture Courses for manufacturers and operatives, and for research work and training scholarships.

To attain these objects the Livery has already been greatly strengthened by the election of influential and prosperous men, mainly recruited by the Master amongst his friends and business connections, in London and the Provinces, and to these it is now proposed to add from time to time those actually engaged in the Glass Industry, and to form a Reconstruction Committee consisting of some members of the Court, with the addition of those Liverymen who have practical knowledge of the Glass Industry.

An interesting development of this movement is well described in the following account in the " Times " Trade Supplement for October, 1918 :—

Before the War this country was very largely dependent upon Germany and Austria for its glassware. In the scientific branches of the trade it was almost entirely at the mercy of our present enemies, but in no industry has greater energy been shown in making up the leeway resulting from long years of neglect.

Prior to the War optical glass was made in this country only by Messrs. Chance Bros., nearly all our requirements were supplied from Jena. The chemicals and scientific glassware industry was practically non-existent. In table glass the trade was gradually being lost. Most of our sheet glass came from Belgium and the United States. Most of our electric light bulbs and lamp chimneys came from Germany and Austria. The best class of white glass bottles were all imported ; even the common bottle trade was largely in foreign hands.   In fact it has been stated that prior to the War only 20 per cent. of the glassware used in this country was made at home.

After the outbreak of war the two immediate needs were chemical glass and optical glass.   Toward the production of the former the way was paved by the Glass Research Committee of the Institute of Chemistry, ably led by Professor Sir Herbert Jackson. Subsequently the formation of the Optical Munitions Branch of the Ministry of Munitions, under the control of Mr. A. S. Esslemont, led to further progress.

The Department of Glass Technology was founded in the University of Sheffield in 1815, and later was supported by the Department of Scientific and Industrial Research, by the Ministry of Munitions, and by the Glass Manufacturers.   Dr. Turner, Director of the Department of Glass Technology at Sheffield University, to whom we are indebted for much of the information now published, has declared that since 1916 manufacturers have " rapidly progressed from a state of despondency to one of determined optimism." Co-operation has replaced secretiveness, and a number of new trade associations have sprung up, such as the British Chemical Ware Manufacturers' Association, the British Laboratory-Ware Association, the British Flint Manufacturers' Association, and the British Lampblown Scientific Glassware Manufacturers' Association.   In eighteen months the Society of Glass Technology has gathered 350 members.

Great progress has been made in the manufacture of optical glass, chemical glass, scientific and surgical glass apparatus and instruments, electric light bulbs, and the production of preserving dishes and jars.   For all-round purposes British-made flasks, beakers, and similar apparatus are second to none in the world.   The light blown scientific apparatus, graduated apparatus, ampoules, syringes, dolls' eyes and artificial human eyes are all products of a glass blowing industry introduced since the war.

Professor P. G. H. Boswell has shown that this country is far better off in glass-making sands than was thought.   New and valuable fireclay deposits have been brought to light, new glass furnaces have been erected, new machinery installed.   The future is full of promise.   Everywhere there is a determination to succeed.   Co-operation between masters and between masters and men, more attention paid to technical research, more outlay on the technical training for craftsmen—these are the foundations on which the trade must and will be based, if it is to flourish " root and branch."

With a view to further development on these lines the Glaziers' Company invited those taking a prominent branch in the glass industry to a Luncheon, held at Painters' Hall last month, as a preliminary to a representative meeting of all interested in the trade to be held in London this month, when it is hoped to bring about closer relations.

The Master, Mr G. P. Walford, presided, and among those present were :— Sir Harry Foster (the Upper Warden), Mr. C. W. Grimwade (the Renter Warden), Mr. Percy Tippetts (the Clerk), Professor W. Ripper (Vice-Chancellor of the University of Sheffield), Lieut.-Col. H. K. Stephenson, D.S.O. (Senior Pro-Chancellor of the University of Sheffield), and Messrs. E. Manville (President of the Association of

Chambers of Commerce), A. J. Hobson (Junior Pro-Chancellor of the University of Sheffield), J. Hasselbee (Secretary of the National Flint Glass Makers' Society), S. W. Morrison, O.B.E. (Technical Director, Optical Munitions and Glass War Supply Department), Dr. W. E. S. Turner (Director of the Department of Glass Technology, University of Sheffield), Major G. D. Hazzledine (Secretary of the Glass Trades Interim Industrial Reconstruction Committee), R. S. Biram (Chairman, Inter-Departmental Glass Trades Committee), etc.

In welcoming the guests, the Chairman said that the ultimate object was to create a central organization to promote the production of glass and glassware to supply our own needs, and not only to prevent for ever the competition of German glass in this country, but also to compete in foreign markets.

In replying, Professor Ripper emphasized the need for co-operation and the value of scientific work to the industry. He paid a tribute to the work of Dr. Turner, and expressed appreciation of the cordial manner in which the glass industry had supported him.

Lieutenant-Colonel Stephenson said that the work undertaken by the University of Sheffield was not purely local, but extended to all parts of the country.

Mr. C. J. Hobson spoke of the establishment of the tungsten industry in Sheffield after the outbreak of war and referred to the fact that when these works were opened it was necessary to use German glass in the Chemical Laboratory because none other was obtainable. To-day they could use British glassware. Our enemies, he said, had made this War a war of engineering and science. We had accepted the challenge and there was no point in which we had not beaten him. The difficulties which still faced us could be solved by getting together and devoting ourselves heartily to overcoming them.

Dr. Turner referred to the work of the training schools and emphasized the importance of technical training both for craftsman and for works management going hand in hand with scientific research.

Another important and attractive feature in the modern life and future activities of the Company is the fraternal action of the Worshipful Company of Stainers in offering to the Glaziers' Company on very acceptable terms the use of Painters' Hall as their future home. This old Hall, rebuilt after the Fire of London, is a beautiful example of the Renaissance of the Seventeenth Century, and with its windows of stained glass and stately array of paintings of Past Masters and works of English Art, leaves an indelible impression on the memory of those who enjoy hospitality under its roof.

Finally, in order to provide the funds necessary for carrying out these objects, the Master has started a special fund, which has already been generously supported, and which will appeal to the sympathy of all who wish well to the Company, and it is hoped that wealthy members will not only aid it during their lifetime, but will make generous bequests to it, and so add their names to the Roll of its Benefactors, as a record for all time.

It may be added, for the information of those desirous of joining the Glaziers' Guild, that the fees and fines payable on joining the Company amount in all to £35 14s. 2d. and thereafter there is only an annual payment of 4s. under the name of quarterage.

A function of peculiar interest to the Glaziers' Company has occurred as we go to press.   On 8th October, 1918, a presentation was made at the Guildhall to Sir Harry Seymour Foster, J.P., D.L., Upper Warden of the Company, the reproduction of whose photograph occurs facing p. 2.   It consisted of an antique clock and a loving cup, and was the appreciation of the energy and enterprise manifested by the recipient in the defence of the Livery Franchise on behalf of an influential body of Liverymen.

The success of the movement, necessarily modified by the existing circumstances, was undoubtedly due to the Upper Warden, and the Company is to be congratulated upon numbering among its members such an energetic champion of the City privileges.

CHAPTER XII.

DEEDS BOOKS, ETC., IN THE COMPANY'S POSSESSION.

Bound in Parchment.

Copies of Wills of various benefactors of the Company, with leases, etc., of the property left bequeathed, and at the sale of the Queen Street property to the Corporation.

Minute Book, 25 January, 1697, to 21 Sept., 1720. (Very bad condition.)

Minute Book, 30 November, 1742, to 10 December, 1760. (With Clasps.)

Minute Book, 5 October, 1799, to 20 November, 1815. (With Clasps.)

Minute Book, 25 April, 1859, to 30 November, 1888.

Renter Warden's Account Book, 1781 to 1894 (With Clasps. Requires renovation.)

Bound in Leather.

Copy upon vellum of Charter of Charles I, and also of the Loriners' Hall Bye-Laws.

Orphan Book or Apprentice Book from June 29, 1694, to July 8, 1836, with receipts of fees by Chamberlain of London. (With Clasps.)

Orphan Book, 1836 to 1854. (With Clasps.)

Freeman's Admission Book, 30 July, 1729, to 25 January, 1794. (With Clasps.)

Bound in Tooled Leather.

The Loriners' Hall Bye-Laws engrossed upon parchment (*vide* page 130).

Lists of Liverymen entitled to Vote, 1832 to 1842.

Bundle of Summonses, various dates.

Clerks' Agenda Notes, 1864 to 1873.

Sundry Documents, Notices of Meetings, etc. (Richard Dann and C. H. Lovell, Clerks).

Insurance Policy and Receipts, 1804 ; Mr. Hardman's Vouchers, etc., *circa* 1804 to 1817.

Sundry Letters (— Lovell, Clerk).

Proceedings in Parliament, 1886, and various Letters.

Quarterage Books, 1792 to 1817.

      ,,   ,,   1798 to 1822.

      ,,   ,,   1860 to 1870.

Bundle of Wardens' Vouchers, 1820 to 1830.

Voting Lists, Vouchers, 1844 to 1861.

Printed Lists of the Livery, 1807 to 1917 (various years).

Livery List, 1720 to 1912.

Minute 8 January, 1761, to 21 September, 1779.

Minute Book (current), 25 January, 1889.

Renter Warden's Book, 25 January, 1895, to 9 November, 1910.   (Bound in red morocco.)

Charter of James II.   1685.

Deeds, Parchments, etc., as enumerated in Chapter V.

THE CHARTER OF KING CHARLES I.

(6 November, 1638.)

Charles by the grace of God King of England Scotland ffraunce and Ireland Defender of the Fayth, etc. **To All** to whom these presents shall come Greeting **Whereas** we are informed by the humble petition of our well-beloved subiects the ffraternity of the Mistery or Arte of Glaziers of our Citty of London That divers persons using the Trade of Glasyers and Painters of Glasse in or neare the Citty of London have for many yeares past and still doe use and practice many abuses and deceipts in that Trade in the draught of their lead beyond the proportioned length for the weight thereof in keeping of rules of a prohibited length in working of false and deceitfull materialls and in handling the same falsely to the great abuse of our Subjects and the scandall of the Arte or Mistery of Glasyers **And Whereas** the petitioners though they have been an auncient ffraternity and have heretofore made many good orders for the regulation of themselves and their Trade which have from time to time been ratified by the Courte of Lord Maior Aldermen and Comon Councell of the said Citty and approved of and enlarged in many particulars in the Reignes of severall Princes by sundry decrees in the High Court of Starchamber have not sufficient power and authority for that they are not sufficiently incorporated to make due search and scrutiny and to correct false materialls or the persons using them now to order and governe the particular Members of their ffraternity as other Companies have and enioy **Wherefore** they most humbly besought us to graunt them our Royale Charter for incorporating the present ffreemen of that Trade within the Citty of London and five miles compasse of the same into one Body Corporate or Politique by the name of the Wardens and Commalty of the Mistery or Arte of Glasiers and Painters of Glasse of the City of London to have perpetuall succession with certeyne powers of or electon admission and swearing their Maister two Wardens foure and twenty Assistants and other inferior Officers from time to time and with some ordinary Clauses and Rules for the well Governing themselves and their Trade and for purchasing of Lands in Mortmain to the value of fforty pounds per Annum And that wee would bee pleased to confirme unto them the same and such like reasonable Customes Decrees Ordinances ffrancheses and priviledges which they now doe and formerly have enioyed by what name and by what lawfull meanes soever And to give them power for the future in their Assemblies to make anie other reasonable Orders and Statutes for the rule and good government of their Society their Trade and all persons useing the same and to impose punishment by Fine or otherwise upon offenders and to levy such ffines to the use of the Company And that none henceforth should sett upp or use the said Trades of Glasing or painting of Glasse or worke therein otherwise than as a servant to a ffreeman unles they had served as Apprentices to ffreemen of the said Mistery **Know yee therefore** that wee being graciously inclined to the humble petiton of our said Subjects in the premisses and for the better reformacōn of the falseties and abuses now frequently practised in the said Trade to the Comōn damadge of our people and for the good governement and regulation of the said Arte or Mistery and the persons using the same in a iuste and orderly way Of our especiall grace and certeine knowledge and meere motōn have willed ordained constituted and granted and by these presents for us our heires and Successors doe will ordaine Constitute and grant that That Thomas Kirbishire, John Rowse, Robert Braitwaite, John Butterfield, William Herbert, Isaacke Bungard, John Dynes, Abaticek Kirbie, John Richards, John Addison, Richard Butler, Thomas Richards, John King, Edward Ffigge, William Hide, John Sanderson, Christopher Hewett, Richard Campion, Daniell Burton, Eusebius Palmer, Baptist Sutton, Nicholas Banister, John Bargeman, and John Smith, being Glasiers and Ffreemen of our said Citty of London and all such others being Ffreemen of London as now doe or may use the said Arte or Misterie of Glasiers and Painters of Glasse in the said Citty of London and within three miles compasse thereof for ever hereafter be and shall bee by vertue of these presents one Bodie Corporate and Politique in deed and in name and shall have continuance for ever by the name of Maister Wardens and Commālty of the Arte or Mistery of Glasiers of the Citty of London we doe by these presents for our heires and successors really and fully create make ordeine constitute confirme and declare to bee one Body Corporate and Politique to have continuance for ever. And that by the same name they may and shall have perpetuall Succession And that they by the name of Maister Wardens and Commālty of the Arte or Mistery of Glasiers of the Citty of London shall bee for ever hereafter personeable and capable in law to purchase have receive and enioy Mannors meassuages Lands Tenements Liberties priviledges jurisdictions ffranchises and other hereditaments whatsoever of what kind nature or quality soever they be to them and to their Successors in fee and perpetuity or for Tearme of life lives or yeares or otherwise in what sorte soever not held of us our heires or Successors in Capite or by Knights service nor any other person or persons whatsoever by Knights service And alsoe all manner of Goods Chattels and Things whatsoever of what name nature or quality soever they bee And alsoe to give grant lett assigne aliene sett over and dispose of any Mannors Messuages Lands Tenements and hereditaments Goods or Chattells And likewise to doe performe and execute all and singular other Art and Arts whatsoever by the name of Maister Wardens and Commālty of the Arte or Mistery of Glasiers of the Citty of London And that they or their Successors by that name shall and may be able to plead and bee impleaded to answeare and be answered unto defend and bee defended in what Court or Courts soever and before any judge or justice and other persons and Officers of we our heires and Successors whatsoever in all and singular actōns Pleas suits Plaints matters and demands of what kind quality or sorte soever they shal bee in the same and in as ample manner and forme as any other of our Subiects of this our Realme of England being able and capable in the Law or any other Body Corporate and Politique within this our Realme of England can own may have purchase receive possess enioy reteyne give grant lett alien dispose and assigne implead or bee impleaded answeare or bee answeared unto defend or be defended do performe or execute   And that they the said Maister Wardens and Cominalty of the Arte or Mistery of Glasiers of the Citty of London and their Successors shall and for ever hereafter have a Comōn Seale to serve and use for all causes things matters and affairs whatsoever of them and their Successors   And that it shall and may bee lawful to and for them and their Successors to alter and make new the said Seale from time to time att their wille and pleasures as they shall think fitt.   𝕬𝖓𝖉 𝖋𝖚𝖗𝖙𝖍𝖊𝖗 wee will and ordaine And by these presents for us our heires and Successors doe give and graunt unto the said Maister Wardens and Cominalty of the Arte or Mistery of Glasiers of the Citty of London and their Successors full power and authority to assemble themselves and meete togeather from time to time in some convenient place within the said Citty of London where they shall think most meete and that then and there they shall and may elect and chuse one of the Arte or Mistery in manner and forme hereafter in these presents mentōned which shall be and shall be called the Maister of the said Company of Glasiers of the Citty of London.   And alsoe that then and there they shall or may elect and chuse two of the said Company of Glasiers in manner and forme here-after mentōned which shall be and shall be called the Wardens of the said Company of Glasiers of the Citty of London and alsoe that then and there they shall or may nominate elect and chuse one and Twenty meete persons of the said Commālty in manner and forme hereafter in these presents expressed to be nominated and chosen which shalbee and shalbee called the Assistants of the said Company of Glasiers who from time to time shall bee aiding and assisting to the said Maister and Wardens for the time being in all causes matters and things touching or concerning the saide Company   𝕬𝖓𝖉 𝖋𝖚𝖗𝖙𝖍𝖊𝖗 we doe grant for us our heires and Successors by these presents that the said Maister Wardens and Assistants of the said Arte or Mistery of Glaziers of the Citty of London for the time being or the greater parte of them (whereof the Maister and one of the Wardens aforesaid for the time being to bee two) shall and may have full power and authority by vertue of these presents to make ordaine constitute appoint and sett downe from time to time such reasonable Acts Ordinances Orders and Constitution in writing whatsoever which to them or the greatest part of them whereof the Maister and one of the Wardens as aforesaid for the time being to bee two shall seem fitt good wholesome honest necessary and convenient according to their discrecōns as well for and concerning such oathes as shall bee for to bee administered to the Maister Wardens and Assistants or any other of the said Commālty and for touching and concerning the said Arte or Mistery of Glasiers and Painters of Glasse within the said Citty of London and within three miles thereof as also for the punishment and reformacōn of such deceipts and abuses as from time to time shall or may bee practiced in the said Arte or Mistery within the said Citty or any other place within three Miles thereof   𝕬𝖓𝖉 alsoe for the good rule and Government of the Maistre Wardens Assistants and Commālty of the said Glasiers of the City of London and their Successors and all and singuler persons using or executing the Arte or Mistery aforesaid within the said City or within three miles compasse thereof in all matters and things touching or any wise concerning the same and for declaration after what manner order and forme the said Maister Wardens

Assistants and Cominalty and all and every other person or persons using and executing the said Arte or Mistery within the places aforesaid shall behave demeane carry and use themselves in their said Arte and Mistery for the publique good and profitt as well of our Subjects in general as of the said Maister Wardens and Cominālty and their Successors and for all other matters and caises touching or concerning the said Arts or misteries And whensoever the said Master Wardens and Assistants for the time being or the greater part of them (whereof the Master and one of the Wardens for the time being be two) doe make ordeine constitute and establish such Acts Ordinances Orders and Constitutions to provide and limitt such reasonable paines penalties and punishments either by imprisonment ffines Amerciament or any other lawfull waies or meanes whatsoever uppon all offendors or Breakers of such Acts Ordinances and Constitucōns And that then or att any time after the said Master Wardens and Commalty and their successors shall and may by vertue hereof have levy and take by distress or other lawfull waies or meanes the said ffines and Americiaments to their owne use without the lett or hinderance of us our Heires or Successors or without the giving or rendring any Accompt or other thing to us our Heires or Successors in that behalfe.   All which Acts Ordinances Orders and Constitucōns soe as aforesaid to bee made   We will shallbee observed obeyed performed and kept under the paines and penalties therein to bee conteyned So as alwaies such Acts Ordinances Constitucōns ffines and Amerciaments bee reasonable and not repugnant or contrary to the Laws or Statute of this our Realme of England nor to the Customes or Usage of our City of London   𝔄𝔫𝔡 𝔣𝔲𝔯𝔱𝔥𝔢𝔯 for the better executing our Grant in that behalfe we have treated assigned named constituted appointed and made and by these presents our heires and successors doe assigne create constitute appoint and make our wellbeloved Subject Thomas Kerbishire to be the first and present Maistᵉʳ of the said Company of Glasiers of the Citty of London and to continue in the said office from the date of these presents untill the Feast Day of Saint Matthew which shallbee in the Yeare of our Lord God One thousand six hundred Thirty and Eight if he shall so long live and from thenceforth untill one other shalbee chosen and sworne unto the said Office of Maister of the said Company in due manner according to the Ordinances and Provisions hereafter in in these presents mentioned and expressed he the said Thomas Kerbishire taking his Corporall oath before the Wardens and Assistants for the time being or the greater parte of them for the due and faithfull execution of the said Office or place of Master To which said Wardens and Assistants for the time being or the greater parte of them We doe hereby for us our heires and Successors give power and authority to administer and give the said Oath to the said Thomas Kerbishire the now Maister of the said Company according to the intent and meaning of these presents 𝔄𝔫𝔡 also wee have assigned named ordained constituted and made and by these presents for us our heirs and Successors doe assigne ordaine constitute and make our wellbeloved Subjects Nicholas Banister and John Smith to bee the first and present Wardens of the said Company of Glaziers and that they and either of them respectively to continue in their said office from the date of these presents untill the said Ffeast of

St. Matthew which shalbee in the yeare of our Lord God one Thousand Six hundred thirty eight if the said Nicholas Banister and John Smith or either of them respectively shall soe long live   And from thenceforth untill two others bee chosen and Sworne unto the said office of Wardens of the said Company of Glasiers according to the Ordinances and Provisions herein expressed and declared the said Nicholas Bannister and John Smith taking their Corporall oaths before the Maister and Assistants for the Time being or the greater parte of them whom wee doe hereby authorize to administer the said Oathes accordingly   And wee likewise have assigned constituted and appointed and by these presents for us our heires and Successors do assign name constitute make and appoint our welbeloved Subiects John Rowse, Robert Braitwaite, John Butterfeild, William Herbert, Isaack Bungard, John Dynes, Abaticek Kirby, John Richards, Jonn Addison, Richard Butler, Thomas Richards, John King, Edward Figge, William Hide, John Saunderson, Christopher Hewett, Richard Campion, Daniell Burton, Eusebius Palmer, Baptist Sutton and John Bargeman to be the first and present Assistants of the said Company of Glasiers of the said Citty of London and to continue in the said office of Assistants during their natural lives unless they or any of them respectively shall be removed for misbehaving of him or themselves in the said Office or for some other iust and reasonable cause they taking their Corporall oaths before the said Maister and Wardens before named for the faithfull executon of the said places of Assistants Which said Maister and Wardens wee doe hereby Authorize to administer the same oathes accordinglie. And wee will And by these presents for us our heires and Successors do graunt unto the said Maister, Wardens, and Cominalty of the said Arte or mistery of Glasiers of the Citty of London and their Successors that the said Maister Wardens and Assistants of the said Company for the time being or the greater parte of them (whereof wee will that the Master and one of the Wardens for the time being to bee two) from time to time for ever hereafter shall have full power and authority yearly and every yeare att and upon the Feast day of Saint Mathew to elect and nominate one of the Wardens or Assistants for the time being to bee Maister of the said Company for one whole year from thence ensueing and from thence untill one other of the said Wardens or Assistants shalbee elected and sworne according to the ordinances and provisions in these presents expressed and declared.   And that hee which shall be soe chosen and named unto the said office of Maistre of the said Company before hee bee admitted to execute his said office shall take his Corporall oath before the last Maistre and Wardens of the said Company for the time being or any two of them to whome we give powers by these presents to administer the said oath well and truely to execute the said office of Maistre of the said Company in all matters and things belonging to the said office   And that after the said oath Soe as aforesaid to bee taken hee shall have and exercise the said Office of Maistre for one whole yeare from thence next ensuing and from thence untill one other bee chosen and sworne in the said Office in forme aforesaid   And likewise that att the same time of electing the said Maister as aforesaid they may alsoe elect chuse two other of the

Assistants of the said Cominalty of Glaziers of London which shall bee Wardens of the said Company for one whole yeare from thence next ensueing and from thence untill two others of the said Assistants bee chosen unto the said Office as Wardens of the said Company of Glasiers as aforesaid according to the Ordinances and Provisions in these presents expressed and declared. And that they which shalbee soe chosen and named to the office of Wardens of the said Company of Glasiers of the said Citty of London before they be admitted to exercise the office of Wardens shall likewise take their Corporall oathes before the last Maistre and last Wardens of the said Company or any two of them To whom wee give power by these presents to administer the said oath well and truly to execute the said office of Wardens in and by all things touching and concerning the said Office And that after such oathes Soe as aforesaid taken they shall and may execute the said Office for one whole year then next ensuing and from thence untill two other bee chosen and sworne in forme aforesaid unto the said Office of Wardens of the said Company of Glasiers in manner and forme in these presents expressed and declared 𝕬𝖓𝖉 𝖋𝖚𝖗𝖙𝖍𝖊𝖗 by these presents for us our Heires and Successors we will and grant unto the said Maister Wardens and Commialty of Glasiers of the Citty of London and their Successors That if it happen the Maister and Wardens [of] the said Commialty for the time being or any of them att any time within one yeare after that they or any of them be chosen into his or their office or offices to die or to be removed from his or their said Office or Offices which said Maister and Wardens for iust and reasonable cause we will shalbee from time to time amoveable that then and soe often it shall and may bee lawfull to and for such and soe many of the said Maister Wardens and Assistants which shalbee then living or remayning or the greater parte of them atte their Wills and pleasures to chuse make and sweare one other or others of the said Assistants for the time being to bee Maister Warden or Wardens of the said Company according to the orders and provisions before in these presents expressed and declared to execute and exercise the said Office of Maister or of Warden or Wardens of the said Company untill the said feast day of Saint Mathew the next following and from thence untill some other meete and discrete person and persons shalbee elected and sworne into the same Office or Offices. He or they first taking his or their Corporall oath or oaths in manner and forme as is thereinbefore expressed and soe as often as cause shall require. 𝕬𝖓𝖉 𝖋𝖚𝖗𝖙𝖍𝖊𝖗 we will and by these presents for us and our heires and Successors doe grant unto the said Maister Wardens and Cominalty of the Arte or Mistery of Glasiers of the Citty of London and their Successors That whensoever it shall happen any of the Assistants of the said Company for the time being to dy or bee removed from his or their office or Offices which Assistant and every or any of them we will and shall be removeable and be removed by the greater parte of the said Maistre Wardens and Assistants of the said Company for the time being for evill governement or misbehaviour or for any other iust and reasonable cause that then and soe often it shall and may be lawfull to and for the said Maister Wardens and residue of the said Assistants for the time being which shall then survive or remaine or the greater parte of them atte their wills and pleasures from time to time to chuse and name one other or more of the said Commialty as aforesaid being meete and discreete person or persons to bee Assistant or Assistants of the said Commialty in his or their place or stead which shall soe happen to dy or bee removed as aforesaid. And that hee or they after they shalbe soe chosen or named to bee Assistant or Assistants of the said Company as aforesaid before that hee or they or any of them bee admitted to his or their execution of the said office of Assistant or Assistants shall take his or their Corporall oath or oaths before the Maister or Wardens and Assistants of the said Company or the greater parte of them. To whom by these presents wee give power and authority to administer the said oath well and truly to execute the said office or offices and soe as often as the case may require **And further** we doe for us our heires and Successors give and grant unto the said Maister Wardens and Cominalty and their Successors full power and authority that the Maister Wardens and Assistants of the said Company or the greater parte of them shall and may from time to time nominate elect constitute and make one meet and fitt person to be Clarke of the said Company and one other meet and fitt person to bee Beadle of the same to be serviceable and attendant on the said Master Wardens and Assistants of the said Company in all Matters and Affaires touching the said Company And the same Clarke and Beadle or either of them for reasonable cause to displace and amove at the discretion of the said Maister Wardens and Assistants or the greater parte of them for the time being and to administer meet oath or oaths to them for the due and faithfull execution of their said places **And forasmuch** as wee are informed that greate deceipts and abuses are often used committed and done by divers Glasiers and Painters of Glasse in and about the Citty of London who for the most parte make their workes very unsufficiently and deceiptfully to the great losse and hinderance of our Subjects **Wee therefore** intending the speedy reformacōn of the said deceipts and abuses doe further will And by these presents for us our heires and Successors grant to the said Maister Wardens and Cominalty of the saide Arte or Mistery of Glasiers of the Citty of London and to their Successors for ever That it shall and may bee lawfull to and for the said Maister and Wardens of the said Company for the time being or any two of them togeather with two or more of the Assistants for the time being from time to time hereafter when as often as to them shall seeme meete to have the full search veiue tryall and oversight in all fitt and convenient manner within our said Citty of London and Suburbs thereof and within three miles of the said Citty as well of and for all and all manner of worke of Glasse and Painting of Glasse that shall from time to time bee made wrought and putt to sale within the same and whether the lead used in and about the same would be not extended or drawne beyond the proportioned length for the weight thereof And whether the rules by which they worke bee of a iust and due length and whether their works and manufacture bee well and workman like handled and wrought in and by all things and not to the deceipt or abuse of our Subiects. And if upon search so made there should be found anie such deceiptfull workes or manufactures That then the said Maister Wardens and Assistants shall or may deface or destroy the same And the offendor or offendors therein to be further punished by such fine or amerciament as shalbee meete in that behalfe according to the Orders and

Ordinances of the said Company to be made and provided in that behalfe 𝔄𝔫𝔡 𝔣𝔲𝔯𝔱𝔥𝔢𝔯 of our especiall grace certaine knowledge and meere mocōn we have granted and given licence And by these presents for us our heires and Successors do grant and give licence to the said Maister Wardens and Cominalty of the Arte or Mistery of Glasiers of the Citty of London and their Successors That they and their Successors shall and may lawfully purchase receive take and enioy to them and their Successors for ever Mannors meassuages lands Tenements and Hereditaments with their appurtenances within the Realme of England Soe as the same do not exceed the cleere yearely value of fforty pounds per Annum   And that the same be not houlden of us our heires or Successors in Capite by Knights' Service the statute of nott putting lands or tenements to Mortmaine or any other Act Statute Ordinance or Provision to the contrary in anie wise notwithstanding 𝔄𝔫𝔡 𝔣𝔲𝔯𝔱𝔥𝔢𝔯 wee doe for us our heires and Successors grant and confirme to the said Maister Wardens and Cominalty of the Arte or Mistery of Glasiers of the City of London and their Successors that they and their Successors shall and may from henceforward from time to time for ever hereafter have hold use and enioy to them and their Successors all and singular the same and such like reasonable Customes Ordinances ffranchises powers priviledges exceptions jurisdictions and authorities whatsoever which they the said Maister Wardens and Cōialtie now have and enioy or which they or their Predecessors or the Freemen of the said Arte or Mistery by what name or names soever and by what ffraternity or Guild soever or by pretext of what Corporation ffraternity or Guild soever heretofore have used had professed held or enioyed or ought to have used had professed or enioyed by pretext of any Charters or Letters Patents by us or any of our progenitors or Predecessors Kings or Queens of England in any mañer of wise heretofore made granted or confirmed or by vertue colour or pretext of any Orders and Decrees heretofore made and provided by the High Court of Starchamber or by any Acts or Orders made or confirmed by the Court of Maior Aldermen or Comōn Councell of our said Citty of London or by any other lawfull meanes right Custome use prescriptōn right or title whatsoever heretofore used had or accustomed Any Statute Act Ordinance matter cause or thing to the contrary thereof in any wise notwithstanding 𝔄𝔫𝔡 𝔚𝔢𝔢 further will and by these presents for us our heires and Successors do graunt to the Wardens and Cominalty of the Arte or mistery of Glasiers of the City of London and their Successors by vertue of these presents for the better worke and working in the aforesaid Arte or Mistery for their Comon Benefitt of our Subjects for that the said Arte or Mistery of Glaziers and Painters of Glasse is a manuall Arte.   That from henceforth it shall not be lawfull for any Person or Persons whatsoever to sett up use or exercise the Arte or Mistery aforesaid within the Citty of London or the liberties thereof or to worke or make any of the worke or working in anie wise touching or concerning the same Artes or Misteryes within the same Citty or liberties thereof otherwise than as Servant or Servants to a Freeman of the said Company unles hee or they have been first brought up in the same Arte as Apprentice or Apprentices to a ffreeman of the said Company by the space of Seaven yeares at the least under peine of the displeasure of us our heires and Successors.   And further for his or their contempt in the premisses to bee punished according to the laws and statutes of this Realme and the Customes of our Citty of London and the Ordinance made or to bee made by the aforesaid Maister Wardens and Assistants of the said Company unles it bee by the Widdows of ffreemen of the said Citty and such as are free thereof by Patrimony **And wee** doe further for us our heires and Successors will require authorize and comãnd all and singular Maiors Sheriffs Justices of Peace Bayliffs Constables Headboroughs and others the Officers and Ministers of us our heires and Successors whatsoever in all and every place and places whatsoever as well exempt as not exempt within our said Cittie of London and the Suburbs and the Liberties thereof and within Three miles of the same that they and every of them att all time and times hereafter and from time to time upon reasonable request to them or any of them to bee made in that behalf bee furthering helping aiding and assisting to the said Maister Wardens and Cominalty and their Successors in the doing executing and performing of all and singular the Grants powers priviledges and other premisses according to the tenor true intent and meaning of these presents **Although** expresse mencõn of the true yearely value or certeinty of the premisses or any of them or of any other Guifts or Grants by us or by any of our Progenitors or Predecessors to the said Maister Wardens and Cominalty of Glaziers of the City of London heretofore made in these presents is not made or any Statute Act ordinance Provision Proclamacõn or Restraint to the contrary thereof heretofore had made ordained or provided or any other thing cause or matter whatsoever in any wise notwithstanding **In Witness** whereof wee have caused these our Letters to bee made Patents **Witnes** our selfe att Westminster the Sixt day of November in the Thirteenth yeare of our Reigne. [A.D. 1638] per breve de privato Sigille, Wolseley.

GLASIERS CHARTER. (1685. 1 James II. March 18.)

JAMES the second by the Grace of God of England Scotland France and Ireland King defender of the faith etc.   To all to whome these Pr̃sents shall come Greeting WHEREAS the Master Wardens & Com̃onalty of the Art or mistery of Glasiers of our City of London have surrendred all their powers Franchises Liberties priviledges and authorities of or concerning the electing nominating constituting being or appointing of any person or persons into the severall offices of Master Wardens Assistants and Clarke of the said Company wch surrender we have accepted and do hereby accept   NOW KNOW YEE that Wee of our especiall grace certain knowledge and meer motion have willed ordained constituted and granted and by these presents for us our heires and successors doe will ordein constitute and grant That all and singular the ffreemen of the Art or mistery of Glaziers of our City of London and suburbs of the same for ever hereafter be and shall be by vertue of these presents one body corporate and Politique indeed and in name and shall have continuance for ever by the name of Mr Wardens and Com̃onalty of the Art or mistery of Glaziers of the City of London and them by the name of Mr Wardens and Com̃onalty of the Art or Mistery of Glaziers of the City of London   Wee doe by these pr̃sents for us our heires and Successors really and fully create make ordeine constitute confirme and declare to be one body corporate and politique to have continuance for ever and y^t by the same name they may and shall have perpetuall succession   And that they by the name of Mr Wardens and Com̃onalty of the Art or mistery of Glaziers of the City of London shall be forever hereafter persons able and capable in Law to purchase have receive and enioy Manors Messuages Lands Tenem^{ts} Liberties Priviledges Jurisdic̃c̃ons Franchises and other hereditam^{ts} whatsoever of what kind nature or quality soever they be to them and their successors in ffee or perpetuity or for terme of life lives or yeares or otherwise in what sort soever   And also all mañer of goods chattells and things whatsoever of what name nature or quality soever they be And also to give grant lett assigne alien set over and dispose of any Mañors Messuages lands Tenem^{ts} and hereditam^{ts} goods or chattels   And likewise to doe performe and execute all and singuler other Art and Arts whatsoever by the name of M^r wardens & Com̃alty of the Art or Mistery of Glaziers of the City of London And y^t they and their successors by that name shall and may be able to plead and be impleaded to answer and be answered unto defend and be defended in what Court or Courts soever and before any Judge or Justice and other persons and officers of us our heires and successors whatsoever in all and singular Ac̃c̃ons Pleas Suites matters and demands of what kind quality or sort soever they be in the same and in as ample mañer and forme as any other of our subiects of this our Realm of England being able and capable in the Law or any other body corporate and

politique within this our Realm of England can or may have purchase receive
possesse enioy retaine give grant lett alien dispose and Assigne implead or be
impleaded answer or be answered unto defend or be defended doe performe or
execute   And that the s^d Mr Wardens and Comonalty of the Art or mistery of
Glaziers of the City of London and their successors shall and may for ever hereafter
have a Com̃on seale to serve and use for all causes things matters and affaires
whatsoever of them and their successors   And y^t it shall and may be lawfull to and
for them and their successors to alter and make new the s^d Seale from time to time
at their Wills and pleasures as they shall think fitt ;   AND FURTHER we will
and by these presents for us our heires & successors doe grant to the aforesaid
Mr Wardens and Com̃onalty of the Art or mistery of Glaziers of the City of London
and to their successors   That from henceforth for ever there may all shall be one
of the Com̃onalty of the Art or mistery aforesaid in mañer as hereafter in these
presents is menc̃oned to be chosen who shall be and shalbe named M^r of the s^d Art
or mistery of Glasiers   And also that likewise there may and shall be two of
ye Com̃onalty of the Art or mistery afores^d in mañer as hereafter in thesee presents
is menc̃oned to be chosen which shalbe and shalbe named Wardens of the Art or
mistery of Glaziers of the City of London afores^d   And also that there may and
shalbe eighteen or more of the Comonalty of the Art or mistery afores^d to be chosen
in forme hereafter in these presents menc̃oned wch shalbe and shalbe named Assistants
of the Art or mistery of Glasiers of the City of London aforesaid and from time to
time shall be Assistants and helpers to the s^d Master and Wardens for the time
being in all causes businesses and matters touching the s^d Com̃onalty of ye Art or
mistery of Glasiers   AND FURTHER we will and by these presents for us our
heires and successors do grant to the afores^d Mr Wardens and Com̃onalty of the Art
or mistery of Glasiers of the City of London and their successors   That the Master
Wardens and Assistants of the Art or mistery afores^d for the time being or the
greater part of them whereof wee will that ye M^r and one of the Wardens for the
time being be two upon publick sumñons thereof to be made being for y^t purpose
met togeather may and shall have full power & authority to make constitute & ordein
from time to time Lawes Statutes & Constituc̃ons Decrees and ordinances reasonable
in writing whatsoever wch to them or the greater part of them (whereof wee will
that the M^r & one of the Wardens for the time being be two) shall seem to be good
wholsome profitable honest and necessary according to their sound discretion for
ye good rule and governm^t of the s^d Mr Wardens and Com̃onalty of the Art or
mistery afores^d and all and singuler other persons the said Art or mistery of Glaziers
within the City of London afores^d the Liberties and precincts of the same exercising
and occupying   And for declarac̃on in what mañer and order the same Mr Wardens
and Assistants and all and singular officers and ministers of the Art or mistery
afores^d in their offices Functions ministeries Arts and businesses within the City
afores^d and the Libties and precincts of the same for the time being shall behave
carry and demeane themselves for the further publick good com̃on profitt and good

governm^t of the Art or mistery afores^d and for all other matters & causes whatsoever the said mistery or Art afores^d touching or in anywise concerning　And that the said Mr Wardens and Assistants of the Art or mistery afores^d for the time being or the greater part of them (whereof we will that the M^r and one of the Wardens for ye time being be two) as often as they shall make ordeine or establish such Lawes Institucõns rights ordinances and constitucõns in forme afores^d such and the like paines punishm^{ts} & penalties by ffines and amerciam^{ts} ag^t and upon all offending against such lawes rights ordinances and constitucõns or any of them wch to the s^d Mr Wardens and assistants for the time being or the greater part of them (whereof wee will that the M^r and one of the Wardens for the time being be two) shall seem most necessary fit and requisite for the observing of the same Lawes ordinances and constitucõns to make ordein limitt and provide　And the same ffines and amerciam^{ts} they shall and may levy take by distresse and have to the use of the said Master Wardens and Society and their Successors without any interrupcõn of us our heires or Successors or of any officers or ministers of us our heires or Successors or without any account to us our heires or Successors to be therefore rendred　All and singuler wch ordinances rights and constitucõns soe as afores^d to be made wee will shall be observed under the paines in the same to be contained Soe that such Lawes ordinances constitucõns ffines & amerciam^{ts} be reasonable and not repugnant nor contrary to the Lawes Statutes Customes or rights of our Realm of England or the Customes of Our City of London　And for the better execution of our Will in this behalfe Wee have assigned named created constituted and made and by these presents for us our heires and Successors doe assigne name create constitute and make our Wellbeloved John Oliver Esqr to be the first and moderne Master of the Art or mistery of Glasiers of the City of London to continue in the s^d office of M^r of the s^d Art or mistery from the date of these presents unto the ffeast of St Mathew next after the date of these presentes and from thence untill one other fitt person unto the office of M^r of the Art or mistery afores^d shall be elected and preferred if the said John Oliver shall soe long live　And we have assigned named created constituted and made and by these presents for us our heires and Successors doe assigne name create constitute and make our welbeloved Richard Dutton and Thomas Tipping Junr to be the two first and modern Wardens of the said Art or mistery of Glaziers of the City of London to continue in the afores^d office of Wardens of the afores^d Art or mistery from the date of these presents untill the s^d Feast of St. Mathew next coming and from thence untill two other unto that office of Wardens of the s^d Art or mistery shall be elected and preferred according to the ordinances and provisions in these presents expressed and declared　If the s^d Richard Dutton and Thomas Tipping Junr shall soe long live　And we have assigned named created constituted and by these presents for us our heires & Successors doe assigne name create and constitute our welbeloved William Rider Thomas Hide Daniel Davis Samuel Rainger Thomas Savage ffrancis Good Willm̄ Stratford Robert Todd Matthias Smith Richard Woodland Henry Anger Willm̄

Woodroffe Thomas Sarney William Price John Hill Edward Avery Willm̄ Carter
& Willm̄ Ireland to be the first & moderne Assistants of the Art or Mistery
of Glaziers of the City of London aforesaid to continue in the said Offices
during their naturall Lives Unles in the meanetime for ill government or ill
behaving themselves in that behalfe or for any other reasonable Cause they or
any of them shall be removed   AND WEE FURTHER will & by these
presents for us our Heires & Successors doe grant unto the said Master
Wardens & Coïalty of the said Art or Mistery That as often as it shall
happen any of the Master Wardens or Assistants or Clerke for the time being
to dye or to be removed that then & in every such Case some other fit
person or persons shall from time to time be elected constituted & sworne
into the said Office or place Offices or places of any such person or persons
so dead or removed by such persons and in such manner & forme as hath
heretofore bin usuall & customary in the said Company   AND OUR
FURTHER pleasure is & wee doe by these presents for us our Heirs &
Successors grant to the said Wardens and Society of the Art or Mistery of Glaziers
of the City of London & their Successors That they & their Successors for henceforth for ever may & shall have one honest & discreet person to be Clerke to
the said Master Wardens & Cöialty of the said Art or Mistery and for the better
Execuc͂on of our will herein wee have assigned nominated constituted & appointed
.& by these presents for us our Heirs & Successors doe assign nominate constitute
& appoint our welbeloved James Oliver to be Clerke to the said Master Wardens
and Com̄onalty of the said Art or Mistery AND WE FURTHER will & by these
presents comand and ordeyne that the Master & Wardens in these presents before
named and constituted before they or any of them be admitted to execute their
respective Offices doe take the severall Oaths com̄only called the Oaths of Allegiance & Supremacy and the oathes prescribed and menc͂oned in an Act of Parliam^t
for the well governing and regulating of Corporations made in the thirteenth
year of the reign of the late King Charles the second our dearly and entirely
beloved brother of blessed memory togeather with the usuall oathes of M^r and
Wardens for the due execuc͂on of their respective offices and also that they and
every of them shall subscribe ye declarac͂on prescribed and menc͂oned in the
afores^d Act for the s^d Wm Rider and Thomas Hide or either of them whom we
direct and appoint by these Letters Pattents and doe give and grant power
and authority to give administer and require the severall oathes and subscripcon
aforesaid in the Court of Assistants of the said Company And wee also will and
firmly comand and enioyne that the severall Assistants and Clarke in these
presents named & constituted before they or any of them be admitted to the
execucon of their offices respectively that they and every of them respectively
shall take the s^d oaths of Allegiance and supremacy and the oathes prescribed
and menconed in the afores^d Act togeather with the severall oathes of Assistants and Clark of the s^d Company for the due execucon of the offices of

Assistants and Clark of the s^d Company and subscribe the declaracon afores^d before the M^r & Wardens herein named or either of them whom we direct and require by these Letters Pattents and doe give and grant power and authority to give administer and require the severall oathes and subscripcon afores^d in ye Court of Assistants of the s^d Company   PROVIDED ALWAYES and our Will is and by these presents for us our heires and Successors wee charge and comand that noe person or persons at any time hereafter shall be elected nominated and put into the office or offices of Mr Wardens Assistants or Clark of the said Company who before his or their respective eleccon doe or doth not hold comunion with the Church of England and within six months before such eleccon have not or hath not rec^d the Sacrament according to the forme of the Church of England by law Established and that all and every person and persons after such eleccon and before his admission in or to the offices or places afores^d shall each and every of them take the s^d severall oathes of Allegiance and Supremacy and the oathes prescribed and mencöned in the afores^d Act togeather with the usuall oathes of the Master Wardens Assistants and Clark of the s^d Company respectively for the due execucon of their respective offices   And that each and every of them shall subscribe the declaracon afores^d before the last M^r and Wardens of the said Company or any two of them for the time being which s^d severall oathes and subscripcöns Wee direct and require and by these presents for us our heirs and Successors to give and grant to them power and authority to give administer and require in ye Court of Assistants of the s^d Company from time to time as often as occasion shall require, ALSO we will and comand that every Clark to the Society of the s^d Art or mistery of Glaziers hereafter to be nominated and chosen before he be admitted into such place or office shall be presented to us our heires or Successors to be approved by us our heires or Successors   And if Wee our heires or Successors shall approve of such Clarke under our Privy Signett or Royall signe Manuall that then he taking the severall oathes aforesaid and making the declaracon and subscripcon before mencöned shall be thereunto admitted   But in case Wee our heires or Successors shall refuse the approbacon of such person so chosen to be Clark y^t then every such eleccon shall be void and the Mr Wardens and Assistants for the time being or the maior part of them in the Court of Assistants shall imediatly proceed to the electing another person to be their Clark who shall be presented as afores^d for the like approbacon and soe from time to time untill such person shall be chosen who shall be approved by us our heires or Successors as afores^d and shall take the s^d severall oathes and make the s^d subscripcon PROVIDED alwayes and we further Will and declare that every eleccon of Mr Warden Assistant or Clark of the s^d Company contrary to the direccöns limitacöns in these presents in that behalfe mencöned shall be void and of none effect to all intents and purposes whatsoever   PROVIDED alwayes and by these presents Wee will and declare that it shall and may be lawfull for us our Heires and Successors from time to time and all times hereafter by order made in the privy Councell of us our heires or Successors from time to time to remove and declare to be removed any Mr Warden Assistant or Assistants or Clark of the s^d Company now or for the time being and thereupon the place or office of such person soe removed or declared to be removed shall be ipso facto void and one or more fit person or persons shall in due mañer be elected constituted and sworne in the place or places of such person or persons soe removed or declared to be removed as aforesaid according to the order and provision afores^d which s^d person or persons soe to be chosen shall before hee or they be admitted into such place or office each and every of them take the severall oathes and make the subscripcon afores^d and soe as often as the case shall thus happen AND FURTHER we will and comand for us our heires and Successors that the Mr Wardens and Coñonalty of the s^d mistery and their Successors be from time to time and at all times hereafter subiect and obedient to the Lord Maior and Court of Aldermen of the City of London for the time being in all things that concerne the good governm^t of the City of London PROVIDED alwayes and our Will also is that noe person or persons of the said mistery for the time being who shall not hold coñunion with the Church of England or shall frequent or be present at Conventicles or any unlawfull assembly under pretext of religious Worship shall at any time hereafter be chosen or brought upon the Livery of the s^d Company when the same shall be granted to the s^d Company by the Maior and Court of Aldermen of the said City of London and that every person chosen or to be chosen upon the Livery of the s^d Company before he be thereunto admitted shall be approved by the Lord Maior and Court of Aldermen of the City of London and shall take the s^d oathes of Allegiance and Supremacy and the oathes prescribed and mencõned in the s^d Act for well govr'ing and regulating of Corporacõns And shall make the s^d subscripcõns before the M^r and Wardens of the s^d Company or any two of them in a Court of Assistants which s^d M^r and Wardens or any two of them for ye time being in the Court of Assistants wee doe by these presents for us our heires and Successors order authorise and require to give & require the s^d oathes and subscripcõn as afores^d PROVIDED further and Wee doe for us our heires and Successors declare that if any person or persons who were of the Assistants of the said Company at the time of the surrender afores^d shall not within the space of three monthes after the date of these presents surrender his or their office or place of Assistant or Assistants of the s^d Company to the Mr Wardens and Coñonalty of the said Art or mistery and submitt to a new elecĉon at the pleasure of the s^d Company then every such person shall not nor ought to have any power or priviledge in or concerning the electing any officer or officers member or members of the s^d Company but shall thereof and of and from all benefitt of this our grant be wholly discharged and excluded AND for the reformacõn & prevencõn of all deceipts and abuses that may or shall be used coṁitted or practized in the s^d Art or mistery within the s^d City of London the Liberties and precincts of the same we doe further Will and by these presents for us our heires and Successors grant to the said Mr Wardens & Coṁonalty of the said Art or mistery of Glaziers of the City of London and their Successors for ever that it shall and may be lawfull to and for the M^r and Wardens of the s^d Company for the time being or any two of them together with two or more of their Assistants for the time being from time to time hereafter when and as often as to them shall seem meet to have the full view search triell and oversight in all fitt and convenient mañer within our s^d City of London and suburbs thereof and within five miles of the said City as well of and for all and all mañer of works of glasse & painting of glasse that shall from time to time be made brought and putt to sale within the same and whether the Lead used in and about the same worke be not extended and drawn beyond the proporc̃oned length for the weight thereof And whether the rules by wch they worke be of a iust and due length and whether their workes & manufacturers be well and workemanlike handled and wrought in and by all things and not to the deceipt or abuse of our Subiects And if upon search soe made there shall be found any such deceitfull workes or manufactures that then the s^d Mr Wardens and Assistants shall and may deface and destroy the same and the offender or offenders therein to be further punished by such ffine or amerciam^t as shall be meet in that behalfe according to the order and ordinances of the said Company to be made and provided in that behalfe   AND FURTHER of our especiall grace certain knowledge and meer moc̃on Wee have granted and given license and do by these presents for us our heires and Successors Do give and grant license to the s^d Mr Wardens and Coṁonalty of the Art or mistery of Glaziers of the City of London and their Successors that they and their Successors shall and may lawfully purchase receive take and enioy to them and their Successors for ever Mañors messuages Lands tenem^ts and hereditam^ts with their appurtences within ye Realme of England soe as the same doe not exceed the clear yearly value of one hundred and fifty pounds per añ   The Statutes of not putting lands or Tenem^ts into mortmain or any other Statute Act ordinance or provision to the contrary in any wise notwithstanding AND further wee doe for us our heires and successors grant and confirm to the said Mr Wardens and Coṁonalty of the Art or mistery of Glaziers of the City of London and their Successors That they and their Successors shall and may from henceforwards from time to time forever hereafter have hold use and enioy to them and their Successors all and singuler the same and such like reasonable customes ordinances Franchises powers priviledges exempc̃ons iurisdicc̃ons and authorities whatsoever wch they the s^d Mr Wardens and Coṁonalty now have and enioy or which they or their Predecessors or the ffreemen of the said Art or mistery by what name or names soever and by what ffraternity or Guild soever or by pretext of what corporac̃on Fraternity or Guild soever heretofore had used possessed held or enioyed or ought to have used had possessed held or enioyed by pretext of any Charter Letters Patents by any our Progenitors or Predecessors Kings or Queens of England in any mañer of wise heretofore made granted or confirmed or by any other lawfull meanes right Custome or prescripcon right or Title whatsoever used had or accustomed and not otherwise in these presents altered limited or appointed any Statute Act ordinance matter cause or thing to the contrary thereof in anywise notwithstanding, AND we furtherwise and by these presents for us our heires and successors doe grant to the Mr Wardens and Coñonalty of the said Art or mistery of Glaziers and their Successors that from henceforth it shall not be lawfull for any person or persons whatsoever to sett up use or exercise the Art or mistery aforesaid within the City of London or the Liberties thereof or to worke or make any of the works or working in any wayes touching or concerning the same Art or mistery within the same City or Liberties thereof otherwise then as servant or servants to a Freeman of the said Company unless hee or they have bin first brought up in the same Art as Apprentice or Apprentices by the space of seaven yeares at the least unles it be by the widowes of Freemen of the s^d City and such as are Free thereof by Patrimony AND Wee will and by these presents for us our heires and Successors do grant to the said Mr Wardens and Coñonalty aforesaid that all and every person now useing or exercising or that shall hereafter use or exercise the Art or mistery of Glaziers as well within our s^d City of London the Liberties and precincts thereof as within any other place or places within five miles of the said City and who now are or hereafter shall be ffree of any other Company or Companies of the s^d City shall hereafter bind or cause to be bound all and every their Aprentices at the hall and to one or more of the members or Freemen of the s^d Company of Glaziers and such Apprentices shall also make Free or cause to be made or admitted ffree of the said Company IN WITNES whereof wee have caused these our Letters to be made Pattents WITTNES our selfe at Westminster the eighteenth day of March in the first year of our reigne.

By writt of privy Seal   PIGOTT.

Pro fine in Hanaperio vi^{li} xiii^s iiii^d

ACTS, ORDINANCES, BYE LAWS, ORDERS AND CONSTITUTIONS
MADE BY THE
MASTERS, WARDENS, AND ASSISTANTS OF THE ART OR MYSTERY OF
GLAZIERS AND PAINTERS OF GLASS OF THE CITY OF LONDON
At a COURT OF ASSISTANTS held at LORINERS' HALL, London,

on the Nineteenth Day of February in the Twenty Third Year of the Reign of our Sovereign Lord George the Second by the Grace of God of Great Britain, &c., and in the Year of Our Lord One Thousand Seven Hundred and Forty Nine.

———————

1. Court of Assistants appointed.

How to be summoned.

It is ordered, That the Master, Wardens, and Assistants of the Company for the Time being, or the Greater Part of them (whereof the Master and One of the Wardens of the said Company, for the Time being, to be Two) shall, and may assemble themselves, and meet together, from Time to Time, in such convenient place within the City of London where, and so often as they shall think meet, on Two Days notice in Writing, first left at the Habitations of the Master, Wardens, and of all their Assistants of the said Company, then known to reside within the City of London, or the Liberties thereof ; and shall be called and taken to be a Court of Assistants of the said Company ; and shall and may make, appoint, and set down, from time to time, such Ordinances & Orders in Writing, as to them or the greater Part of them, shall seem fit, good, necessary, and convenient, according to their Directions ; and consult of, and manage the Affairs and Business of the said Company.

How often to be held.

And that the said Court of Assistants shall be summoned, called, and held, Four times at the least in every Year (that is to say) on the Feast of the Conversion of St. Paul the Apostle being the 25th Day of January ; on the Feast of St. Mark the Evangelist, being the Twenty-fifth day of April ; on the Feast of St. Peter the Apostle, being the Twenty-ninth Day of June ; and on the Feast of St. Matthew the Evangelist, being the Twenty-first Day of September, or on the Morrow of such of the said Feasts as shall or may happen on a Sunday, or on such other Days before or after any, or either of the said Feasts, as the said Master, Wardens, and Assistants of the said Company, or the greater part of them shall or may at any Time, for just and reasonable Cause, think fit to order and appoint.

2. Master and Wardens to take an Oath of Office.

The office to continue for one year.

Also it is ordered, That every Person and Persons, who shall be named and chosen to the general offices of Master and Wardens of the said Company, before they be admitted to execute the said several Offices of Master and Wardens, shall take the Oaths hereafter mentioned, before the last Master and Wardens of the said Company, or any Two of them, and after such oath so as aforesaid taken, they shall and may execute the said several Offices for one whole Year, then next ensuing ; and from thence, until others be chosen and sworn in form aforesaid, into the said several Offices of Master and Wardens of the said Company.

Also it is ordered, That every Person that shall hereafter be nominated and elected to be Master, or One of the Wardens, of the said Company, shall yearly, and every Year, on the Feast of Saint Andrew the Apostle, being the Thirteenth day of November (or on the Morrow if the said Feast shall happen on a Sunday) or on such other Day as shall be for that Purpose agreed upon and appointed by the Master, Wardens, and Assistants of the said Company, or the greater Part of them, appear before the said Master, Wardens and Assistants of the said Company, or the greater Part of them, at a Court of Assistants by them to be held at the meeting place of the said Company in London, in order to be sworn, and take upon him such of the said Offices of Master, or one of the Wardens of the said Company, to which he shall have been so nominated and elected; and in Case any Person so nominated and elected to be Master, or one of the Wardens of the said Company, being duly summoned to take upon him the said office of Master or Warden (shall neglect or refuse to appear, pursuant to the said Summons, or having appeared, shall neglect or refuse to be sworn into and take upon him such of the said Offices to which he shall have been so nominated and elected) not having a reasonable Cause for such his neglect or refusal, he shall forfeit and pay to the Use of the said Company, the several and respective Sums of Money hereafter mentioned; If a Master the sum of TEN Pounds; if an Upper Warden the sum of FIFTEEN Pounds; and if an Under Warden the sum of TWENTY Pounds; and every such Person shall be likewise dismissed, discharged, and removed from being an Assistant of the said Company, if the Master, Wardens, and Assistants of the said Company, or the greater Part of them, as a Court of Assistants, by them to be held, shall, in their Discretion, think fit, and so order and determine.

3. Master and Wardens to account.

Master or Wardens refusing the office.

If Master to pay £10; if Upper Warden to pay £15; if Renter Warden £20 and may be dismissed the Court.

Also it is ordered, that the Under Warden of the said Company for the time being, shall be, and shall be called Renter Warden of the said Company; and that every Person that shall be nominated and elected to be Renter Warden of the said Company, before he shall be sworn into, or take upon him the said Office of Renter Warden, shall pay to the Renter Warden of the said Company for the time being, or to such Person or Persons as by the said Master, Wardens and Assistants of the said Company, or the greater Part of them, shall, in that Behalf be ordered and Appointed to the Use of the said Company, the sum of FOUR Pounds THIRTEEN shillings and FOUR pence, of lawful money of Great Britain; and shall also enter into Bond to the said Company in Six Hundred Pounds, or such other reasonable and sufficient Penalty as shall be appointed and settled by the Master, Wardens and Assistants, or the greater Part of them, from Time to Time, as Occasion shall require, with condition thereto as hereafter followeth: viz.

4. Renter Warden to pay a fine of £4. 13. 4.

And give a Bond to account, &c.

" Whereas the above Bound A.B. hath been lately chosen Renter Warden of the Company of Glaziers, London; and is now about to take upon him that Office : Now the condition of the above written Obligation is such that if the above Bound A.B. his Executors or Administrators do, and shall, on the Feast of Saint Andrew the Apostle which shall be in the Year of Our Lord one thousand Seven Hundred and . . . . (or on the Morrow of the said Feast) or upon such other day as shall be agreed upon

Conditions of the Bond.

and appointed by the Master, Wardens, and Assistants of the said Company, or the greater Part of them, for the swearing the next succeeding Master and Wardens of the said Company into Office, or within One Month after the Determination of the Office of Renter Warden of the said A.B. by Death, Removal, or otherwise, present, exhibit, make and deliver to the Master, Wardens, and Assistants of the said Company, or the greater Part of them, at such Place as shall be by the said Master, Wardens and Assistants, or the greater Part of them, for that purpose, appointed, a just, true and faithful Account and Reckoning in Writing of, and concerning all such Receipts and Payments as the said A.B. shall have made in, and during the Time of his being Renter Warden of the said Company, in order that the said Account may be by them examined, audited, summed up and allowed : And also do, and shall then and there, without Diminution, Cover, Fraud, or Delay, well and truly pay, surrender, and deliver up unto the said Master, Wardens & Assistants, or the greater Part of them, or to such Person or Persons, to and for the Use of the said Company, as by the said Master, Wardens and Assistants of the said Company, or the greater part of them, shall, in that Behalf, be ordered and appointed.   Not only the Book and Books of Accounts of the said A.B. and all other Escripts, Evidences, Writings, Muniments, and Books belonging to the said Company : but also, all and singular, such Rents, Money, Stock, Jewels, Plate, Bonds, Bills, Cash, Notes, or other Securities, Escripts, Evidences, Writings, Utensils, Implements of Household Keys ; and all other goods, Chattels, and Things, whatsoever, which shall, by and after such Account so made, examined, audited and allowed, be found to remain, and be in his or their Hands, Custody, Charge, or Power of, or belonging to the said Company ; then this Obligation to be void, or else to be or remain in, full Force and Virtue.''

If any Person that shall be so nominated and elected to be Renter Warden of the said Company, shall neglect or refuse to pay the said Sum of Money before mentioned to be paid, or to enter into such Bond as aforesaid, every such neglect or refusal in either of the above Cases, shall be deemed and taken to be a refusal of the said Office ; and every Person so Offending, shall forfeit and pay to the Use of the said Company the sum of TWENTY Pounds, and shall likewise be dismissed, discharged, and removed from being any longer an Assistant of the said Company (unless just Cause be shown to the Contrary ;) if the Master, Wardens, and Assistants, or the greater Part of them, at a Court of Assistants, by them to be held shall, in their Discretion, think fit and so order and determine.

5. Renter Warden to have a Surety.   Also it is ordered, That every person that shall be so nominated and elected to be Renter Warden of the said Company shall procure, or cause, One sufficient Surety to be approved by the said Master, Wardens and Assistants of the said Company, or the greater Part of them, to become bound together with such Renter Warden elect, jointly and severally, in the said Bond, so as aforesaid, to be entered into by him to the said Company, under such Penalty and with such Condition, as aforesaid for the due Execution of this said Office, and together with such Renter Warden elect, to subscribe, seal,

and as his Act and Deed, sufficient in Law to deliver the same ; and that such Renter Warden elect, within Fourteen Days after his Election into the said Office, shall leave in writing with the Clerk of the Company for the Time being, the Name, Place of Abode and Profession, Trade, or Calling of such Surety, that a proper Inquiry may be made after his Sufficiency ; and if any Person that shall be so nominated and elected to be Renter Warden of the said Company shall neglect or refuse to procure, or cause One sufficient Surety to become bound, together with him in the said Bond, so as aforesaid, to be entered into by him to the said Company, in manner aforesaid, or to leave in Writing the Name, Place of Abode, and Profession, Trade, or Calling of such Surety in Manner above directed (Notice of his Election being given to or left for such Renter Warden Elect, within the space of Seven Days next after such his Election ; if he shall not be present thereat) every such Renter Warden elect so neglecting or refusing as aforesaid, shall not, at any Time while he shall continue in the same Office of Renter Warden, in any ways intermeddle with, or receive, have, or take into his Hands, Charge, or Custody, any of the Rents, Monies, Stocks, Jewels, Plate, Bonds, Bills, Cash, Notes or other Securities, Utensils, Implements of Household, Keys, or other Goods, Chattels, Effects or Things whatsoever, of, or belonging to the said Company ; but that it shall and may be lawful to, and for the said Master, Wardens and Assistants of the said Company or the greater Part of them, from Time to Time, and at all Times, when, and as often as Need or Occasion shall be, or require, to depute, order, and appoint some other Assistant of the said Company to receive, have, and take the same, and every Part and Parcel thereof, to the Use of the said Company.

Also it is ordered That yearly, and every Year, on Saint Matthew's Day being the Day of Election of a new Master and Wardens, or on the next Day if Saint Matthew's Day happen on a Sunday, or on such other Day within Seven Days before or after the said Feast, as shall be by the said Master, Wardens and Assistants of the said Company, or the greater Part of them, agreed upon, and ordered and appointed for just and reasonable Cause for holding the Quarter Day Court of Assistants, a Dinner of Entertainment shall be provided and had at the Charge and Expense of the said Company, for the Master, Wardens, and Assistants thereof ; and that the Renter Warden of the said Company for the time being, shall pay towards the Charges and Expenses of the said Dinner the Sum of FIVE Pounds and FIVE Shillings ; and every Renter Warden of the said Company, who shall neglect or refuse to appear at the Quarter Day Court of Assistants of the said Company, to be held Yearly on Saint Peter's Day, or on the Morrow in case that Day be Sunday, or within Seven Days before or after the said Feast as aforesaid ; or, having appeared shall then and there, neglect or refuse to undertake to charge himself in his Account as Renter Warden of the said Company with the said Sum of FIVE Pounds and FIVE Shillings, or to pay to the Master or Upper Warden of the said Company or such of them as shall be then present for the Use of the said Company, the said sum of FIVE Pounds and FIVE Shillings towards the Charges and Expenses of the said Dinner, at the Election of the said Master, Wardens and Assistants of the

[marginal notes:]
6. Dinner on St. Matthew's Day.

Renter Warden to pay £5 . 5 . 0 towards the Dinner

or forfeit £100.

said Company, or the greater Part of them ; or having undertaken to charge himself in his Accounts as Renter Warden of the said Company, with the said sum of FIVE Pounds and FIVE Shillings, shall afterwards neglect or refuse to pay the same, shall forfeit and pay to the use of the said Company the sum of TEN Pounds.

7. Master and Wardens to Account on S. Andrew's Day.   Also it is ordered That yearly and every year, on the Feast of Saint Andrew the Apostle being the Thirteenth Day of November, or on the Morrow (if the said Feast shall happen on a Sunday) or on such other Day as shall be agreed upon and appointed by the Master, Wardens and Assistants of the said Company, or the greater Part of them, for the swearing the new Master and Wardens into Office ; the old Master and Wardens of the said Company shall, after the swearing of the New Master and Wardens into Office, present, exhibit, make and deliver up to the Master, Wardens, and Assistants of the said Company, or to the greater Part of them, at the Court of Assistants by them to be then held a just, true, and faithful Account and Reckoning of, and concerning all Receipts and Payments, and Disbursements, which shall have been made by the said last Master and Wardens and any or either of them, and of and concerning all Rent, Money, Stocks, Jewels, Plate, Bonds, Bills, Cash, Notes, or other Securities, Escripts, Evidences, Writings, Utensils, Implements of Household ; and all other Goods, Chattels, and things whatsoever, touching and belonging to, concerning or appertaining to the said Company, or which ought to be accounted for by the said last Master and Wardens ; or any or either of them, written and entered in a Book to be provided and kept for that Purpose to be by the said Master, Wardens and Assistants, or the greater Part of them, examined, audited, summed up and allowed, and being so allowed by them, shall be subscribed by them, or the greater Part of them under their Hands ; and the said last Master and Wardens shall have allowed unto them upon such examining, auditing, and summing up of such their Account, all and every such Reasonable costs and Charges, Expenses and Disbursements, as they, or any of them shall have laid out, expended, or disbursed, for or about the necessary Affairs, Occasions, or Business of the said Company ; and after such Account and Reckoning so exhibited, made, and delivered up, and examined, audited, summed up and allowed and subscribed, the said last Master and Wardens shall then and there pay, surrender, and deliver up unto the said Master, Wardens and Assistants of the said Company, or the greater Part of them, or to such Person or Persons to, and for the Use of the said Company as by the Master, Wardens, and Assistants of the said Company, or the greater Part of them, shall, on that Behalf be ordered and appointed, all and every the Monies, Stocks, Jewels, Plate, Bonds, Bills, Cash, Notes, or other Securities, Escripts, Evidences, Writings, Utensils, Implements of Household, and all other Goods, Chattels, and things whatsoever of, or belonging to the said Company, which upon, by, or after such Account and Reckoning so made, examined, audited, summed up, allowed and subscribed, shall be found to remain, and be in their, or any of their Hands, Custody, Charge, or Power ; and every Person who shall offend in any of the Points or Premises aforesaid, contrary to the Tenor and true Intent and Meaning of this present Ordinance, or any Matter or Thing therein contained, shall forfeit and pay

for every such Offence, to the Use of the said Company, the Sum of Ten Pounds of lawful Money of Great Britain.

Also it is ordered, That whensoever it shall happen that any of the Assistants of the said Company for the Time being shall die, or be removed from his or their Office, or Offices, by the greater Part of the said Master, Wardens, and Assistants of the said Company for the time being for evil Government or Misbehaviour, or for any other just and reasonable Cause, that then, and so often it shall and may be lawful to, and for the said Master, Wardens, and residue of the said Assistants for the time being which shall then survive or remain, or the greater Part of them, at their Wills and Pleasures, from Time to Time, to name and choose one other, or more Person or Persons of the Liverymen of the said Company, to be Assistant or Assistants of the said Company, as aforesaid, in his or their Place or Stead, which shall so happen to die or be removed as aforesaid ; and that he or they, shall be so named and chosen to be Assistant or Assistants of the said Company as aforesaid, before that he or they or any of them, be admitted to his or their Execution of the said Office of Assistant or Assistants, shall take the Oath hereafter mentioned before the Master, Wardens, and Assistants of the said Company, or the greater part of them, well and truly to execute the said Office or Offices ; and also shall pay to the Renter Warden of the said Company for the Time being or to such Person or Persons as by the said Master, Wardens and Assistants of the said Company, or the greater Part of them, shall, in that Behalf be ordered and appointed to the Use of the said Company, the sum of THREE Pounds FOURTEEN Shillings and Two-pence : and if any Person who shall be so named or chosen to be Assistant of the said Company having due Notice given to, or left for him, of such Election, and of the Time and Place appointed for his appearing to take upon him the said Office, shall neglect or refuse to appear pursuant thereto, or having appeared, shall neglect or refuse to be sworn into, and take upon him the said Office, or to pay the said Sum of Money above-mentioned (not having a reasonable Excuse for such his Neglect or Refusal) every such Person, in every or either of the said Cases, shall forfeit and pay to the Use of the said Company the sum of TWENTY-FIVE Pounds of lawful money of Great Britain.

Also it is ordered, That in Case any Master, Warden or Assistant of the said Company being duly summoned, should neglect or refuse to appear, and give his Attendance at any Court of Assistants of the said Company, to be called, kept, and holden as aforesaid, before the expiration of One Hour next after the Time appointed, or mentioned in the Summons for holding such Court, or having appeared, shall depart without Leave of such Court before such Court be dismissed, not having a reasonable Excuse ; that then, and in either of the said Cases, every such Person so offending, shall forfeit and pay to the Use of the said Company the several and respective sums hereafter mentioned (that is to say) If a Master or One of the Wardens the sum of Two Shillings and Sixpence and every other Assistant the Sum of ONE Shilling.

Also it is ordered, That the Master, Wardens and Assistants of the said Company shall not reveal any of the private Debates, Resolutions or Orders of the Court of

Marginal notes:

8. Assistants dying or removing.

Court to choose others out of the Livery.

Oath of Assistant.

To pay £3 . 14 . 2 on taking the office.

Refusing to take the office forfeits £25.

9. Master, Wardens, or Assistants not appearing when summoned ;

Or departing the Court without leave, Forfeits if Master or Wardens 2s. 6d., if Assistants 1s. 0d.

10. Assistants revealing Debates of the

Company forfeit First offence 20*s.*, Second offence 40*s.*, Third £5 and his discharge of the Court.

Assistants of the said Company, or any secrets belonging to the said Company unto any Person or Persons whatsoever, not being Assistants of the said Company, and especially not to any such Person or Persons whom the same Matter may in anywise concern or touch, on pain to Forfeit and pay to the Use of the said Company for the First Offence the sum of TWENTY Shillings and for the Second Offence the Sum of FORTY Shillings ; and the Person so offending shall, for the Third Offence, forfeit and pay the sum of FIVE Pounds, and shall moreover be removed and discharged from being any longer an Assistant of the said Company.

11. Assistants absenting 18 successive Calendar Months

Not having been Master or Wardens to pay £15 and may be removed from being an Assistant.

Also, it is ordered, That if any of the Assistants of the said Company do or shall absent himself from the Meetings of the said Master, Wardens, and Assistants of the said Company or the greater Part of them, at the Courts of Assistants, so by them to be called, kept, and held as aforesaid, for the Time and Space of Eighteen successive Calendar Months, being duly summoned and shall not have appeared at any Court of Assistants within that time, every such Assistant in Case he shall not before have passed or served the Office of Master or one of the Wardens of the said Company, shall, for such his Neglect, forfeit and pay to the use of the said Company, the sum of FIFTEEN Pounds ; and it shall and may be lawful to, and for the said Master, Wardens and Assistants, or the greater Part of them, at a Court of Assistants by them to be called and held, and for that purpose specially summoned, to remove every Assistant so absenting from being any longer an Assistant of the said Company, unless he having Notice thereof, shall show sufficient Cause to the contrary.

12. Election of Stewards.

Also, Whereas it hath been accustomed in the said Company to have a Dinner of Entertainment provided for the Master, Wardens and Assistants, and Liverymen of the said Company on the Day of the Lord Mayor's Solemnity, by Stewards chosen annually from Time to Time ; It is therefore ordered, That forever hereafter it shall and may be lawful to and for the Master, Wardens, and Assistants of the said Company for the time being or the greater Part of them, to elect and choose annually Four Persons, such as to them may seem fit, being Members of the said Company, who have not before been Stewards or fined for the same, to be Stewards on the Lord Mayor's Day, to find and provide a Dinner for the said Master, Wardens, Assistants and Liverymen on that Day, at such fit and convenient Place, within the City of London, as shall be yearly at the Time of such Election directed and Appointed ; and every Member so elected and having due Notice given, or left for him, who shall refuse or neglect to appear before the said Master, Wardens, and Assistants or the greater PART of them, at the said Company's Hall, or other place of meeting in London, at the Time of their Meeting next after such Election and Notice as aforesaid, and then and there undertake to serve the said Office and to provide and pay for One Fourth Part of such Dinner of Entertainment, to be made in such manner and according to such Bill of Fare as shall be then and there given not exceeding the Sum of THIRTY Pounds, or in lieu thereof, pay down to the Master

or pay a Fine of £6.

and Wardens or such of them as shall be then present, for the Use of the said Company and as a Fine for being discharged from the Service of the said Office of Steward the Sum of Six Pounds or that having made his Election to serve the said Office, and to provide and pay for One Fourth Part of such Entertainment as aforesaid, shall afterwards neglect so to do, shall forfeitt and pay to the Use of the said Company the sum of FIFTEEN Pounds.

Also it is ordered, That the Master, Wardens, and Assistants of the said Company or the greater Part of them, as often as they shall think fit, shall and may call, nominate, choose, elect and admit into the Livery or Cloathing of the said Company, such & so many Persons, being Freemen of the City of London, and of the said Company as they shall think meet and able to be of the same Livery or Cloathing ; and every Person so called, nominated chosen and elected, shall upon his Admission into the said Livery, or Cloathing, pay to the Master, and Wardens of the said Company, or such of them as shall be then present, or to such Person or Persons as by the said Master, Wardens and Assistants of the said Company, or the greater Part of them shall, in that Behalf, be ordered and appointed for the Use of the said Company, the sum of Six Pounds FOURTEEN shillings and Two-pence of lawful money ; and every Member so called, nominated, chosen and elected into the said Livery or Cloathing and having due notice given to him or left for him at his House or Place of abode of such Election, and of the Time and Place appointed for his appearing to take upon him, and be admitted into the said Livery or Cloathing, who shall refuse or neglect to appear at such Time and Place, and then and there take upon him and be admitted into the said Livery or Cloathing, and pay the said sum of Six Pounds FOURTEEN shillings and Two-pence (not having a just cause or reasonable excuse for such Neglect or Refusal) shall forfeit and pay to the use of the said Company the sum of TWENTY-FIVE Pounds.

Also it is ordered, That every Member of the said Company who doth now or here- after shall use, profess, exercise, or manage either of the Arts or MYSTERIES of Glazing or Painting of Glass, to and for his own proper Gain, Profit or Advantage, as a Master Workman therein, who hath not, or shall not have made, wrought, and presented and struck out, performed, and finished, a Design, Plot or Proof Piece of his Workmanship, in manner hereafter mentioned, shall appear before the Master, Wardens, and Assistants of the said Company, or the greater Part of them, at a Court of Assistants by them to be holden, when for that Purpose duly summoned, and there and then, for the Trial and Approbation of his Skill and Cunning in his Trade aforesaid, make, work, and present, within the Meeting Place of the said Company to the Master, Wardens and Assistants of the said Company or the greater Part of them, a Design, Plot, or Proof Piece of his workmanship, to be by him there struck out, performed and finished according to the Rule and Order of the said Master, Wardens and Assistants for the Time being, or some of them, in that Behalf, to be prescribed and given ; and that no Member of the said Company who doth now or hereafter shall use, profess, exercise, or manage, either of the said Acts or Mysteries of Glazing or Painting of Glass, as a Journeyman therein, who hath not or shall not have already made, wrought, and presented, and struck out, performed and finished a Design, Plot or Proof Piece of his Workmanship in Manner hereinafter mentioned, shall use, profess, exercise, or manage the said Arts or Mysteries, or either of them, to, and for his own proper gain, Profit, or Advantage, as a Master Workman therein, until such Times as he shall, for the Trial and Approbation of his Skill and Cunning in his Trade aforesaid, Make, work, and present, within the Meeting Place of the said Company, to the Master, Wardens and Assistants of the said Company, or the greater Part of them, a Design, Plot, or Proof Piece of his Workmanship to be by him there struck out, performed, and finished according to the Rule and Order of the said Master, Wardens, and Assistants for the time being, or some of them in that Behalf, to be presented and given ; and every Member shall pay for and upon such Approbation, to the Use of the said Company, the sum of NINE Shillings and Two pence of lawful Money towards the charge and Expenses of finding and providing the Materials for doing the same, being the Fees therefore payable according to the antient usage of the said Company ; and every member who shall neglect or refuse to appear before the Master, Wardens, and Assistants of the said Company or the greater Part of them, at any Court of Assistants, by them to be holden when duly summoned for any of the Purposes aforesaid, or shall act contrary to this Ordinance in any of the Points aforesaid, or shall neglect or refuse to pay the said sum of NINE shillings and TWO pence before mentioned, shall forfeit and pay in any or either of the said Cases, for every such Offence, to the Use of the said Company, the sum of FIVE Pounds.

15. The Trade to be carried on in Open Shops, not Private Places. And Whereas, many and daily Abuses are practised and committed both by Glaziers and Glass Painters in their Workmanship and Materials, in working in private Rooms and Chambers, and other retired and remote Places ; for the correcting and avoiding thereof, it is ordered, that no Member of this Company, either before or after his making his Proof Piece and Approbation, shall at any time hereafter, use, manage, or exercise the said Arts, or Mysteries of Glazing or Painting of Glass, or either of them, within the City of London, or within the Distance of Three Miles thereof, to his own Profit, Gain, or Advantage, as a Master Workman in the same Arts or Mysteries, or either of them, unless for, and during all such Time as he shall so use, manage or exercise the same, or either of them, he shall hold and keep constantly One open or public Shop, or Outward Work-Place, exposed and set to the Sight and View of his Majesty's Subjects, or otherwise shall set or place his Sirname, at full Length, and also his Trade, upon or over the Street Door, or upon some other part of the House or Place where he shall inhabit upon the outside thereof ; and upon such place where and in such Manner as the same may be publicly and openly seen, viewed and read ; and every Member who shall offend in any of the Points or Things aforesaid, contrary to the Tenor, true Intent, and Meaning of this Ordinance, shall forfeit and pay to the Use of the said Company, for every such Offence the Sum of Five Pounds.

16. Members not to hawk. And it is ordered, That no Members of the said Company using or exercising of the said Arts or Mysteries of Glazing or Painting of Glass, or either of them, unless such who do, or shall at the same time, hold or keep an open or public Shop or Work-place as aforesaid, shall, at any Time, hereafter, hawk, stray, travel about or wander within or about the City of London, or the Distance of Three Miles thereof, to forespeak, beg, ask, crave, or require, or to perform or do any Manner of Work belonging to either of the said Arts or Mysteries, on Pain, that such member acting contrary to this Ordnance, shall forfeit and pay for every such Offence, the Sum of FIVE Pounds.

And also, Whereas great Deceits and Abuses are often used, committed, and done by divers Glaziers and Painters of Glass, in and about the City of London, who for the most Part, make their Works very insufficiently and deceitfully, to the great Loss and Hindrance of His Majesty's Subjects ; for the Reformation of the said Deceits and Abuses it is ordered that it shall and may be lawful to, and for the said Master and Wardens of the said Company for the Time being or any Two of them together, with Two or more of the Assistants for the time being, from Time to Time hereafter, when, and as often as to them shall seem meet, to enter at any convenient Time in the Daytime, into any House or place of any Member of this Company, where Glazing or Painting of Glass is, or shall be used by any Member of this Company, within the City of London and Suburbs, or within the distance of Three Miles thereof, the Door thereof being open, there to search, view, try, and oversee, in a fit and convenient Manner, all, and all Manner of Works of Glass and Painting of Glass that shall, from Time to Time, be made, brought, and put to sale within the same ; and to see whether the lead used in and about the said Works be not extended beyond the proportioned Length for the Weight thereof, and whether the Rules by which they Work be of a just and due Length ; and whether these Works and Manufactures be well and in a Workmanlike Manner handled and wrought in every respect, and not to the deceit and abuse of His Majesty's subjects ; and if upon search so made there be found any such deceitful Work or Manufactures, or any Lead used or employed, or to be used and employed in the Performance and Despatch of the said Arts or Mysteries, or either of them, drawn or extended beyond the proportioned Length for the Weight thereof, *to wit*, a Quantity of Lead weighing One Ounce, and a Length exceeding the Length of One Foot and Three Inches, or any Rules or Measuring Instruments not of a just Length or Proceeding, but of a defective, false, or prohibited Length, or any Works made or done deceitfully, or with false, unfit, or ill-conditioned materials, or handled or placed abusively. That then and in every or any such Case, it shall and may be lawful to and for the said Master and Wardens of the said Company, for the time being, or any Two of them together, with Two or more of the Assistants for the Time being, from Time to Time, to cut, break, and deface all such Quantities of Lead, and all such Rules and Measuring Instruments of such prohibited Length ; and all such Works so made or done deceitfully, or with false, unfit, or ill-conditioned Materials, or handled or placed abusively ; and every Member that shall offend in any Points or Things aforesaid, contrary to the Tenor, True Intent and Meaning of this Ordinance, or any Part thereof, shall forfeit and Pay to the Use of the said Company, for every such offence, the sum of Ten Shillings ; and every such Person who shall neglect or refuse to pay the same, shall forfeit and pay to the Use of the said Company the sum of FORTY Shillings : and every Member who shall resist the said Master and Wardens of the said Company for the Time being, or any Two of them,

17. Power to Search

and oversee materials in the Trade.

Regulations in Lead Work.

Deceits in Trade.

Penalties on Offenders.

Persons resisting the Search.

coming together, with Two or more of the Assistants of the said Company or any or either of them, or shall refuse to permit or suffer them, or any or either of them, to enter into any such House or Place, or shall refuse to open the Door of such his House or Place where Glazing or Painting of Glass is, or shall be used, when for this Purpose required, here to search, view, try, and oversee, the several Works, Manufactures, Materials, and Things before mentioned, or any of them, or shall in any ways interrupt or hinder them, or any or either of them, in so doing, shall forfeit and pay for

Forfeit £5. every such Offence, to the Use of the said Company, the sum of FIVE Pounds.

18. Persons whose Houses are searched to pay 4d. Also it is ordered, That it shall and may be lawful, to and for the said Master and Wardens of the said Company for the Time being, or any Two of them together, with Two or more of the Assistants for the Time being, to ask, demand, receive, and take, once in every year, at the Time of the First Search (such year commencing from the 25th day of December) the Sum of Four-pence, for every Member whose House or Place where Glazing or Painting of Glass is, or shall be used, they do or shall search as aforesaid and every Member who shall refuse or neglect to pay the same shall forfeit and pay to the Use of the said Company the sum of THIRTEEN Shillings and Four-pence.

19. Election of Clerk and Beadle. Also it is ordered, That the Master, Wardens, and Assistants of the said Company, or the greater Part of them, shall and may from Time to Time, nominate, elect, constitute and make one meet and fit Person to be Clerk of the said Company, and One other meet and fit Person to be Beadle of the same, to be serviceable and attendant on the said Master, Wardens, and Assistants of the said Company, in all Matters and Affairs of the said Company ; and the same Clerk or Beadle, or either of them, for reasonable Cause to displace or remove, at the discretion of the said Master, Wardens, and Assistants, or the greater Part of them, for the Time being, and every Person that shall be so nominated, elected, constituted and made to be Clerk or Beadle of the said Company, before he take upon him such of the said Offices, to which he shall be so nominated, elected and constituted, shall take the Oath in that Behalf, to be administered to him before the said Master, Wardens, and Assistants of the said Company, or the greater Part of them hereafter, for that Purpose, limited and Appointed.

20. Clerk to make all Indentures. Also it is ordered, That the Clerk of the Company for the Time being, or his Deputy, shall make and write all Indentures for Binding every Apprentice, who shall at any Time hereafter, be bound to any Member of the said Company ; and that the said Indenture shall not be made or written by any other Person or Persons whatsoever ; and every Member who shall take any Apprentice who shall be bound in any other Manner, or who shall make or write, or cause any Indentures for binding any Apprentice to himself, to be made or written by any other Person or Persons whatsoever, other than, and except, the Clerk of the Company for the Time being, or his said Deputy, shall forfeit and pay to, and for the Use of the said Company, the sum of FIVE Pounds.

1. Apprentices to be enrolled. Also it is ordered, That every Member of the Said Company (being a Freeman of the City of London) who shall bind any Apprentice to himself, shall, within One Year next after Binding, cause such Apprentice to be presented before the Chamberlain of the City of London for the Time being, to the Intent and Purpose, that he may be inrolled, and shall inroll him, according to the ancient and laudable Custom of the said City, on Pain to forfeit and pay for every such Neglect, so to do to the use of the said Company, the sum of THREE Shillings and Four-pence, and every Member who shall neglect or refuse to pay the same, shall forfeit and pay to the Use of the said Company the Sum of THIRTEEN Shillings and Four-pence.

Also it is ordered, That no Member of the said Company shall, at any Time or Times hereafter, yield, surrender, assign, or turn over, to any Person whatsoever, the Apprentice for the Residue of the Years or Term mentioned in the Indenture, whereby such Apprentice became bound to him, without the Leave, Licence, and Consent of the Master, Wardens, and Assistants of the said Company for the Time being, or the greater Part of them (except by such Order as is hereafter mentioned and expressed) ; and that the same shall always be done by the Clerk of the Company for the Time being, or his Deputy, on Pain that such Member acting contrary thereto, shall forfeit and pay for every such Offence to the Use of the said Company, the sum of FORTY Shillings. *22. Assignment of Apprentices to be made by the Clerk.*

Also it is Ordered, That at the Request of any Member of the said Company, or of any Person desiring to be admitted into the Freedom of the said Company, it shall and may be lawful to and for the Clerk of the said Company for the Time being, in the presence of the Master or Wardens, of the said Company for the Time being, or any of them, or by an Order in Writing, signed by the said Master or Wardens, on One of them, from Time to Time, to bind any Apprentice to any Member of the said Company, or to permit any Member of the said Company to assign or turn over, any his Apprentice to any other Freeman of the City of London, or to administer the Oath of a Freeman hereafter mentioned, to, and to admit any Person into the Freedom of the said Company during the Intervals of any of the Courts of Assistants of the said Company ; and the same shall be as effectual as if done at any Court of Assistants of the said Company and every Person so taking, or assigning, and turning over every Apprentice ; and every Person so admitted into the Freedom of the said Company, shall pay for such private binding, assigning and turning over, or Admission into the Freedom of the said Company to the Clerk and Beadle of the said Company for the Time being, for their extraordinary Attendance and Trouble, the Sum of FOUR Shillings over and above the usual Fees, and every Member who shall neglect or refuse to pay the same, shall forfeit and pay to the Use of the said Company the sum of FORTY Shillings. *23. Private Bindings, Indentures, &c.*

Also it is Ordered, That every Liveryman of the said Company, and every other Person who now is, or hereafter shall be, free of the said Company, who doth, or shall use, manage, exercise, or carry on, any Trade, Art, or Calling, or Profession whatsoever, for his or her own proper Gain, Profit, or Advantage as a Master Workman or Mistress in the same ; and also every other Member of the said Company, not being a Journeyman or Journeywoman, shall pay yearly and every year, unto the said Master and Wardens of the said Company for the time being, to the Use of the said Company at the Meeting *24. Quarterage.*

Place of the said Company, on every of the Four Quarter Day Courts (to wit) on the Twenty-fifth Day of January, the Twenty-fifth Day of April, the Twenty-ninth Day of June, and the Twenty-first Day of September yearly or on the morrow of such of the said Feasts as shall happen on a Sunday, or on such other Day as shall, or may be appointed for just and reasonable Cause, for holding the said Quarter-Day Courts as aforesaid, the sum of ONE Shilling for his or her Quarterage (that is to say) the sum of FOUR Shillings in the whole yearly and every year, and every Member who doth and shall use or exercise any Trade, Art, Calling, or Profession, as a Journeyman or Journeywoman shall pay in like Manner, and on the several Days and at the Place aforesaid, the sum of Six-pence for, and as his or her Quarterage (that is to say) the Sum of TWO Shillings in the whole, yearly and every Year; and he or she who shall neglect or refuse to pay the same accordingly, shall forfeit and pay to the Use of the said Company, for every such Neglect or Refusal, the sum of ONE Shilling.

25. Members Summoned to pay Quarterage.

Also it is Ordered, That every Member of the said Company who shall neglect or refuse to appear before the Master, Wardens and Assistants of the said Company, or the greater Part of them, at any Court of Assistants by them to be holden, whereto he or she shall be duly summoned to pay any Arrears of Quarterage from him or her due, and owing to the said Company or having appeared shall then and there neglect or refuse to pay all Arrears of Quarterage which shall be their due (the same being demanded) ;

To forfeit for 1st Offence 5/- 2nd. 10/- 3rd. 15/-.

shall forfeit and pay to the Use of the said Company for the First Offence the Sum of FIVE Shillings, and for the Second Offence the sum of TEN Shillings, and for every other and subsequent Offence the sum of FIFTEEN Shillings.

26. Members to attend when summoned.

Also it is ordered, That every Member of the said Company shall appear before the Master, Wardens, and Assistants of the said Company, or the greater Part of them, at the Courts of Assistants, by them to be held, when for that Purpose duly summoned ; and every Member who shall neglect or refuse to appear before the said Master, Wardens, and Assistants of the said Company at any Court of Assistants, by them to be held when duly summoned (no lawful Impediment hindering) shall forfeit and Pay to the Use of the said Company for the first default the sum of TWO Shillings and Six-pence, and for every other default the sum of FIVE Shillings.

27. Members to be of civil Behaviour.

Also it is ordered, That every Member of the said Company shall, at all Times, be of good Carriage and civil Behaviour, and demean and behave himself orderly and civilly, both in Word and Deed, towards the Master, Wardens, and Assistants of the said Company, and every of them, in or before their Courts of Assistants, and not to disturb or disquiet any of the said Courts, or wrong, abuse, revile, or evilly intreat any of the Members thereof, or any Persons or Persons resorting to, or attending the same, and be tractable, conformable, and obedient to all and every the lawful Acts, Ordinances, Bye Laws, Orders, and Constitution of the said Company ; and every Member offending in any of the Points or Things aforesaid, contrary to the Tenor, True Intent and Meaning of this Ordinance shall forfeit and Pay for every such offence, to the Use of the said Company, the sum of FORTY Shillings.

Also it is Ordered, That no Member of the said Company, who doth now, or hereafter 28. shall, use or exercise the said Arts or Mystery of Glazing or Painting of Glass, or either of them, within the City of London, or the distance of Three Miles thereof, shall, at any Time hereafter, authorize, permit, or suffer, any Person Whatsoever, not having a Right in that Behalf, or not being duly qualified by the Laws of the Land, or the Laws and Customs of the City of London, so to do, to set up, use, manage, carry on, or exercise, the said Arts or Mysteries, or either of them, by or under his or her Authority, or in his or her name, by or with his or her Consent, Approbation, or Connivance, or shall, by any Ways or Means, whatsoever, teach or instruct, or cause to be taught or instructed, or endeavour to teach or instruct, any Person whatsoever, other than and except the Son of such Member, or his or her Apprentice, lawfully bound or assigned, and turned over to him or her, according to the laws and Customs aforesaid, in the Trade, Art, or Mystery of Glazing or Painting of Glass, or any Skill or Workmanship, or any Thing thereunto relating, or in any wise appertaining, on Pain that such Member acting contrary to this Ordinance, shall forfeit and pay for every such Offence, or in Any or either of the said Cases to the Use of the said Company, the sum of TEN Pounds.

Also whereas the said Art or Mystery of Glaziers and Painters of Glass is a Manual 29. Who may Art, it is ordered, That no Person whatsoever, unless the Widows of Freemen of the carry on the City of London, and such as are free by Patrimony, shall or may set up, use, or exercise, Business. the said Art or Mystery aforesaid, within the City of London, or the Liberties hereof, otherwise than as a Servant to a Freeman of the said Company, unless he hath been, first brought up in the same Art as Apprentice to a Freeman of the said Company, by the space of Seven Years at the least, on Pain, to forfeit and pay for every such Offence, to the Use of the said Company, the sum of TEN pounds.

Also it is ordered, That it shall and may be lawful, to and for the Master and 30. Oaths, Wardens of the said Company for the Time being, or any Two of them, and for the how to be Master, Wardens and Assistants of the said Company for the Time being, or the Administered greater Part of them, from Time to Time, to administer the several Oaths hereafter mentioned, or unto such Persons as shall be admitted unto the Freedom of the said Company, and also, unto the several Persons concerned, and who are mentioned in the same, and in the Acts, Ordinances, Bye-Laws, Orders, and Constitutions before mentioned, or either of them.

Also it is Ordered, That it shall and may be lawful to, and for the Master, Wardens 31. Fines, and Assistants of the said Company for the Time being, or the greater Part of them, to Penalties, &c., mitigate, moderate, and lessen, any of the Fines, Forfeitures, Payments, Pains and mitigated. Penalties herein before set or imposed, in Favour of any Member who shall forthwith pay down such Sum of Money as shall be by them adjudged and thought fit and reasonable to be paid for the Breach of any of these Acts, Ordinances, Bye-Laws, Orders, and Constitutions or any Part thereof.

32. Repeal of
former By-
Laws and how
Fines, Penal-
ties, &c., to
be recovered.

Also it is ordered, That all and every the Acts, Ordinances, Bye Laws, Orders, and Constitutions of the said Company, at any Time or Times heretofore made, shall from henceforth be repealed to all Intents and Purposes ; and that all Fines, Amerciaments, Forfeitures, Payments, Pains, and Penalties before mentioned, shall and may be levied, taken, sued for, and recovered, in the name of the said Company, by action of Debt or any other lawful Ways and Means.

THE OATH OF THE MASTERS AND WARDENS.

You, and each of you, shall swear to be true and faithful to our Sovereign Lord the King's Majesty, that now is, and to his Heirs and Successors, Kings and Queens of this Realm ; and that after the best Manner you can, you shall justly and indifferently execute, or cause to be executed, your several and respective Places, or Offices, of Master and Wardens, of the Company of Glaziers, London ; and in every respect you shall diligently and carefully govern, manage, and carry on their Affairs, and on all Occasions attend the same, during the Time you shall continue in, and execute the said several and respective Places or Offices, you shall conceal their Secrets, and consult their Welfare ; you shall, to the utmost of your Power and Ability, truly and faithfully observe and keep, and cause to be observed and kept, and put in due Execution, all the good and lawful Ordinances made for the good Rule and Government of the said Company, without sparing any Person or Persons for Affection, Reward, Promise of Reward, Dread or Malice ; and you shall duly and well demean yourselves in all things, incident and belonging to the said several and respective Places or Offices.

So help you GOD.

THE OATH OF THE ASSISTANTS.

You shall swear to be true and faithful to our Sovereign Lord the King's Majesty, that now is, and to his Heirs and Successors, Kings and Queens of this Realm ; and that after the best Manner you can, you shall justly and indifferently execute, or cause to be executed, your Place or Office of Assistant to the Master and Wardens of the Company of Glaziers, London : in every respect you shall diligently and carefully govern, manage, and carry on, their Affairs and on all Occasions attend the same during the time you shall continue in and execute the said Place or Office ; you shall conceal their Secrets and consult their Welfare ; you shall to the utmost of your Power and Ability, truly and faithfully observe and keep, and cause to be observed and kept, and put in due execution, all the good and lawful Ordinances made for the Good Rule and government of the said Company, without sparing any Person or Persons for Affection, Reward, Promise of Reward, Dread, or Malice ; and you shall duly and well demean yourself in all things incident and belonging to the said Place or Office.

So help you GOD.

THE OATH OF THE CLERK.

You shall Swear to be true and faithful to our Sovereign Lord the King's Majesty, that now is, and to his Heirs and Successors, Kings and Queens of this Realm ; you shall be obedient to the Master, Wardens and Assistants of the Company of Glaziers, London, for the Time being, in all their just and lawful Commands, relating to the Concerns of the said Company ; you shall attend upon them at all their Courts, Meetings and Assemblies, and make true Entries of all such Matters and things as they shall command to be entered, without respect to any Person or Persons, for Favour, Malice, Dread, or Reward ; you shall deliver out no Copy or Copies of any their Ordinances, nor show any Book or Books belonging to the said Company without the consent of the Master and Wardens thereof for the Time being ; and in all things incident and belonging to the Place or Office of Clerk to the said Company, you shall justly and faithfully demean yourself to the utmost of your Power and Ability.

So help you GOD.

THE OATH OF THE BEADLE.

You shall swear to be true and faithful to our Sovereign Lord the King's Majesty, that now is, and to his Heirs and Successors, Kings and Queens of this Realm ; you shall be obedient to the Master, Wardens, and Assistants of the Company of Glaziers, London, for the Time being in all their just and lawful Commands relating to the Concerns of the said Company : you shall be attendant upon them at all their Quarter Day Courts, and other Courts, Meetings and Assemblies ; you shall from Time to Time, by the Command, and according to the direction of the Master and Wardens, or any of them, summon and warn the Freemen of the said Company, and all things incident and belonging to the Place or Office of Beadle and the said Company you shall well, faithfully, and justly demean and behave yourself.

So help you GOD.

THE OATH OF EVERY FREEMAN.

You shall swear to be true and faithful to our Sovereign Lord the King's Majesty that now is, and to his Heirs and Successors, Kings and Queens of this Realm ; and to be true and just in your Trade, Art, or Calling ; you shall be obedient to the Master, Wardens, and Assistants of the Company of Glaziers, London, and all the good Rules, Ordinances and Orders of the said Company you shall well and truly observe and keep to your Power.

So help you GOD.

Signed this Thirty-First Day of May in the Year of our Lord One Thousand Seven Hundred and Fifty at Loriners' Hall, London, by us

John Stowers *Master.*

Wm. Harris, Jun. }
Adam Dennis   } *Wardens.*

William Harris	Richard Ellis
Boys Waldron	William Hoar
Joseph Cooper	William Keene
Matthew Jarman	Edward Keepe
Thomas Smith	Thomas Lubton
John Greaves	Anthony Seal
Edward Thornton	Thomas Fall
John Corbin	

We, Philip Lord Hardwicke, Baron of Hardwicke, Lord High Chancellor of Great Britain, Sir William Lee, Knight, Lord Chief Justice of His Majesty's Court of King's Bench, and Sir John Willes, Knight, Lord Chief Justice of His Majesty's Court of Common Pleas, in pursuance of the Authority given us by a Statute made in the Nineteenth Year of the Reign of King Henry the Seventh, intituled " An Act for making Statutes by Bodies incorporate " have perused and examined the said Acts, Ordinances, Bye Laws, Orders and Constitutions, and do approve of the same.

Hardwicke, C.
Wm. Lee
J. Willis

EXTRACTS FROM CHARTERS.

Under the first Charter of 1638 the Court had power to make Ordinances, among other things, for the good rule and government of the Masters, Wardens, Assistants and Cominalty of the Company, and for all matters, things and cases touching or concerning the Arts or Mysteries of Glaziers or Painters of Glass in the City of London.

Under the second Charter, granted by James II in 1685, it appears that the old Charter was surrendered and a new Grant made. Under that various powers are given, including one to the Court to make Bye-Laws, for a declaration in what manner the Masters, Wardens and Assistants should behave, carry on and demean themselves for the further public profit and good, and for all other matters and causes the said Mystery or Art aforesaid touching or in any way concerning so that such laws be reasonable and not repugnant nor contrary to the laws of the realm or customary to the City of London.

There were not any other Charters as to the dates of any meetings with the exception of the election of Officers, which has to be on the Feast of St. Matthew, the 21st September.

The Bye-Laws provide that the Court of Assistants shall be summoned four times in every year, viz.: on the Feast of the Conversion of St. Paul the Apostle, the 25th day of January; the Feast of St. Mark the Evangelist, the 25th day of April; the Feast of St. Peter the Apostle, the 29th day of June; and the Feast of St. Matthew the Evangelist, the 21st day of September, or within seven days before or after.

These are the four statutory Courts.

It was provided that the Master Elect shall yearly on the Feast of St. Andrew the Apostle, being the 30th November, appear before the Master, Wardens and Assistants at a Court to be sworn in.

This is therefore the 5th meeting of the Court.

Provides that on the Feast of St. Andrew the Apostle, the 13th day of November (this is obviously a misprint for the 30th) the Court shall meet for the swearing in of the new Master and auditing the Accounts, but there is no provision whatever for the holding of the Court on the 9th November.

Bye-Law 12, however, recites that it has been the custom for the Company to have a Dinner of Entertainment on the Day of the Lord Mayor's Solemnity, and it is therefore ordered that it shall and may be lawful for the Masters, Wardens and Assistants to elect and choose four persons to be Stewards on the Lord Mayor's day to find and provide a dinner for the Master, Wardens, Assistants and Liverymen, and to pay for one fourth of such Dinner of Entertainment, to be made in such manner and according to the Bill of Fare as shall be then and there given, not exceeding the sum of £30, or in lieu thereof to pay as a fine the sum of £6, and if any Steward refuses or omits or neglects to fulfil his duties he shall forfeit the sum of £15.

It will be noticed that this is not obligatory, but that the Court may elect Stewards. The number to be elected was four persons, but this has for some years past been modified by appointing two only.

There does not appear to be anything either in the Charter or the Bye-Laws to make it obligatory to hold either the Court or the Dinner on the 9th November, but the Bye-Laws lay down how such a dinner should be provided if it takes place.

The Bye-Laws could be enforced by a Court of Law, and if any Liveryman were elected a Steward and refused to act, there is no doubt that the fine could be legally recovered so long as the Company acted strictly upon the Bye-Laws, but it is very doubtful indeed whether any Steward could be compelled to make any payment in respect of any dinner held upon any day other than the 9th November, or to pay the fine for not doing so.

The Bye-Laws themselves, which were made in 1750, were approved by the then Lord Chancellor and two Judges, this approval being in accordance with an Act made in the reign of Henry VII. We have referred to this Act to see what would be necessary to be done in case any alteration were made in the Bye-Laws.

The Act, which is intituled 19 Henry VII, chap. 7, provides that no Masters, Wardens and Fellowships of Crafts and Mysteries shall take upon themselves to make Acts or Bye-Laws in disinheritance or against the common profits of the people, but that the same Acts or Ordinances be examined by the Lord Chancellor and two Judges, or the Chief Justice of either Benches, or three of them, under the pain of forfeiture of £40.

It would appear, therefore, that it is only necessary to have the Bye-Law sanctioned if it in any way infringes upon the Royal prerogative or the common weal of the people. It is doubtful whether the present proposition would involve any alteration in the Bye-Laws.

The Court of Assistants ...
other than the Master & Wardens ..

The Father.
Past Master R. Procter

Past Master
Hewlitt

Past Master
Henry Edmunds

Past Master Dyke

Past Master W. J. B. Tippets C.C.

Mr. E. Manville M.P. J.P.

Mr. Enos Howes J.P.

Mr. Arthur
Ritchie Upjohn

Mr. O. H. Pollak

Dr. F. E. Bradley
M.A. M.Com. LL.D. F.R.S.E.

Mr. Bertie Pardoe
Thomas J.P.

Mr. Marshall Stevens
M.P. J.P.

Mr. Charles
Frederick Fenton

1918.

THE MASTER, WARDENS, AND COURT OF ASSISTANTS,

WITH THE LIVERY, OF

THE WORSHIPFUL COMPANY OF GLAZIERS,

KNOWN IN ANCIENT TIMES AS THE

Worshipful Company of Glaziers and Painters of Glass.

Master :

MR. GEORGE PAGET WALFORD,

(FOURTH TIME.)

29, Great St. Helen's, London, E.C. 3, 50, Courtfield Gardens, South Kensington, S.W. 5, and 14, Third Avenue, Hove, Brighton.

Upper Warden :

SIR HARRY SEYMOUR FOSTER, J.P., H.M.L., D.L., Ex-Sheriff of London,

82, Victoria Street, S.W. 1, "Thatched Holm," Wargrave, Berks, and Carlton Club, Pall Mall, S.W. 1.

Renter Warden :

MR. CHARLES WALTER GRIMWADE, F.R.G.S.,

Trafalgar House, 16, Waterloo Place, S.W. 1, and 3, Lombard Street, E.C. 3.

Clerk :

MR. PERCY WILLIAM BERRIMAN TIPPETTS,

11, Maiden Lane, E.C. 4 (Bank 462).

Assistants.

Mr. ROBERT PROCTER, 83, St. Paul's Churchyard, E.C. 4, and 102, Tressillian Road, Brockley, S.E. 4. (*Father of the Company.*)

Mr. CHARLES FREDERICK HEWLITT, "Oaklands," Grove Park, Denmark Hill, S.E. 5.

Mr. HENRY EDMUNDS, M.I.C.E., M.I.E.E., Parliament Mansions, Victoria Street, S.W. 1, and Moulscombe Place, Brighton.

Mr. GEORGE DYKE, 139, Southgate Road, Islington, N. 1, and 27, Cossington Road, Westcliff-on-Sea, Essex.

Mr. WILLIAM JAMES BERRIMAN TIPPETTS, C.C., 11, Maiden Lane, E.C, 4, and Pachesham Lodge, Leatherhead, Surrey.

Mr. ENOS HOWES, J.P., 60, Tabernacle Street, E.C. 2, and 121, Bethune Road, Stamford Hill, N. 16.

Mr. ARTHUR RITCHIE UPJOHN, 6, Stone Buildings, Lincolns Inn, W.C. 2, and "Cranhurst," Surbiton.

Mr. OTTO HERMANN POLLAK, Leadenhall Buildings, E.C. 3, and 18, The Drive, Hove, Sussex.

Dr. FRANCIS ERNEST BRADLEY, M.A., M.Com., LL.D., F.R.S,E., 4, Elm Court, Temple, E.C, 4 ; Bank of England Chambers, Tib Lane, Manchester, and "Stormarn," Chorlton-cum-Hardy.

Mr. BERTIE PARDOE THOMAS, J.P., Trident House, Newport, Mon.

Mr. MARSHALL STEVENS, M.P., J.P., Trafford Hall, and 18, Exchange Street, Manchester.

Mr. CHARLES FREDERICK FENTON, 19, Eastcheap, E.C. 3, and "Claremont," Sunderland Road, Forest Hill, S.E. 23.

Mr. EDWARD MANVILLE, M.P., J.P., 3, Central Buildings, Westminster, S.W. 1., and "Keresley House," nr. Coventry.

Livery.

Mr. HENRY GOODCHILD (*Pensioner*), 73, East Street, Brighton.

Mr. HARRY FENDICK.

Mr. ABNER TORKINGTON.

Mr. EDWARD PALMER.

Mr. CHARLES ROBERT CANN, "Lynton," 17, Wilbury Crescent, Hove.

Mr. PERCY GILLING, Copenhagen Wharf, Limehouse, E. 14, and 14, Boscombe Avenue, Leytonstone.

Mr. LEONARD COATES, 15, Friday Street, E.C. 4, and 84, Park Avenue, Palmer's Green, N. 13.

Mr. WILLIAM LAWRY, "Trevose," Mill Road, Worthing.

Dr. BROUGHAM ROBERT RYGATE, 126, Cannon Street Road, E. 1.

Mr. ERNEST EDWIN LOYD, 15, North Road, Clapham Park, S.W. 4.

Mr. ERNEST NOWILL, 32, Hatton Garden, E.C. 1, and 32, Lancaster Road, West Norwood, S.E. 27.

Mr. BENJAMIN CRUMPLEN.

Mr. WILFRED JOHN CHARLES, 24, College Street, Dowgate Hill, E.C. 4, and 257, South Lambeth Road, S.W. 8.

Mr. WILLIAM CHARLES YOUNG, F.I.C., F.C.S., 24, Aldgate, E.C. 1, and 2, Queen Anne's Grove, Bedford Park, W. 4.

Mr. GRAHAM BUCKLEY, F.R.G.S., 4, Park Place, St. James's, S.W. 1.

Mr. HENRY THOMAS SHEPHERD, George Street, Commercial Road, E. 1, and "Stebonheath," Forest Glade, Leytonstone, Essex.

Mr. FREDERICK DREDGE, 8, Leeside Mansions, Muswell Hill, N. 10.

Mr. WILLIAM BALFOUR CLARKE, "Fulwood House," High Holborn, W.C. 1, and The Cottage, Well End, Bourne End, Bucks.

Mr. JOHN EDWIN BROWNE, 206, Upper Thames Street, E.C. 4, and 16, Cecile Park, Crouch End, N. 8.

Mr. EDWARD SAMUEL SPICER, Thwaite Hall, Erpingham by Norwich, and 73, Philbeach Gardens, Kensington, S.W. 5.

Mr. JOHN ROWAN LINDSAY DAISH, Lyonsdown Works, New Barnet, and 63, High Holborn, W.C. 1.

Mr. ALFRED JAMES MITCHELL, "William the Fourth," Albany Road, Camberwell.

Mr. PERCY WILLIAM BERRIMAN TIPPETTS (*Clerk*), 11, Maiden Lane, E.C. 4, and 76, Longridge Road, Earl's Court, S.W. 5.

Mr. CHARLES HENRY HEATHCOTE, F.R.I.B.A. (*Surveyor*), 110, Cannon Street, E.C. 4; Lloyd's Bank Buildings, King Street, Manchester; 81, Campden Hill Court, W. 8, and "Arnside," Hale, Cheshire.

Mr. NICHOLAS KILVERT, J.P., "Woodcourt," Brooklands, Cheshire.

Mr. ARTHUR FANCE–SPEARE, 42, Pantiles, Tunbridge Wells.

SIR HORACE BROOKS MARSHALL, J.P., LL.D., Temple House, Temple Avenue, E.C. 4, and Shabden Park, Chipstead, Surrey. (*Lord Mayor 1918-19.*)

Mr. WILLIAM RALPH REYNOLDS, "Ellesmere," Kew Gardens, Surrey.

Mr. OLIVER REYNOLDS, "Ellesmere," Kew Gardens, Surrey.

Mr. JAMES EDMUND DYAS, 63, Fore Street, E.C. 2, and 32, Oakwood Avenue, Beckenham.

Mr. SAMUEL ROBERT DYAS, 63, Fore Street, E.C. 2, and Afton Lodge, Ewell Road, Surbiton Hill.

Mr. ALFRED GEORGE JOHN LITTLEWOOD, 9, Derby Road, Tolworth, Surrey.

Mr. HENRY THOMAS CART DE LAFONTAINE, M.A., 52, Albert Court, S.W. 7.

Mr. ALFRED KNIFTON, 17, Hertford Road, Kingsland, N. 1.

Mr. THOMAS HUDDART DONKING, Maritime Buildings, Albert Road, Middlesborough.

Mr. LIONEL FRANK, 29, Great St. Helen's, E.C. 3, and "Hafod," Broxbourne, Herts.

Mr. LEO SUNDERLAND, 47, Victoria Street, S.W. 1.

Mr. GEORGE ARTHUR O'HANLON, 3, Lombard Street, E.C. 3.

Mr. BERNARD AUGUSTUS HOLLAND, 17, Victoria Street, S.W. 1, and 4, More's Gardens, Chelsea, S.W. 3.

Mr. THOMAS STONE, Burrow's Chambers, Swansea, and "Hempstead," Sketty Road, Swansea.

Mr. JOSEPH ROLFE, "Goodig," Burry Port, Carmarthen.

Mr. JAMES JERMYN PRITTY, Park Cottage, Stonehill Road, East Sheen, Surrey, and E. W. Bliss Co., Pocock Street, S.E. 1.

Mr. ERNEST EDWIN SMITH, 23, St. Swithin's Lane, E.C. 4.

Mr. THOMAS ANDREW BLANE, M.P., C.C., 47, Leadenhall Street, E.C. 3.

Mr. CURTIS GEORGE ASHDOWN, C.C., 23, Billiter Street, E.C. 3, and "Glenholme," Plough Lane, Purley, Surrey.

Mr. WALTER DOWDESWELL, 62, Green Street, W. 1, and Bank Buildings, St. James's Street, W. 1.

Mr. LOUIS JOSEPH BIELSKI, Llandough House, Llandough, near Cardiff.

Mr. CHARLES O'MALLEY, 4, St. Mary Axe, E.C. 3.

Mr. FRANK BARNARD SAUNDERS, 26, Martin's Lane, E.C. 1, and "Merthyr House," Bute Docks, Cardiff.

Mr. SIDNEY SANDERSON, 10, Cornfield Road, Eastbourne.

Mr. THOMAS GEORGE OWENS THURSTON, M.I.N.A., M.I.C.E., Vickers House, Broadway, Westminster, S.W. 1.

Mr. FRANK WILFORD MELLOWES, Eclipse Works, Corporation Street, Sheffield, and 6, Taplon House Road, Sheffield.

Mr. GEORGE ARTHUR BROMAGE, 72, Bute Street, Cardiff, and 1, Elston Terrace, Exmouth, S. Devon.

Mr. DIGBY COTES–PREEDY, M.A., LL.M. (Cantab.), L.S.A. (Lond.), Barrister-at-Law, 2, Elm Court, Temple, E.C. 4.

Mr. JOHN HENRY DAVIES, Moseley Hall, Cheadle.

Mr. ROBERT BURDON STOKER, M.P., J.P., "Heatherlea," Green Walk, Bowdon, Cheshire, and 108, Deansgate, Manchester.

Mr. BERNARD JONES, 14, Albion Terrace, Saltburn-by-Sea, and Lloyds Bank Chambers, Middlesborough.

Mr. FREDERICK JONES, 86 & 87, Dock Street, Newport, Mon.

Mr. CHARLES FLETCHER LUMB, 75B, Queen Victoria Street, E.C. 4, and "Hornsby House," Fieldhead, Corkran Road, Surbiton.

Dr. GEORGE TOLCHER ECCLES, M.A., M.B., B.C. (Cantab.), 63, Sackville Road, Hove, Sussex.

Mr. JOSEPH FRAZER, Britannia Buildings, Cardiff, and Park Road, Barry, Glam.

Mr. HUGH ASHLEY LONGBOTHAM, Lindrick Close, Woodsetts, near Worksop, and Carbon Chambers, Water Lane, Sheffield.

Mr. ERNEST MARTIN, 49, Stanwick Mansions, West Kensington, W. 14.

Mr. BERTRAND CHARLES WOTTON, "Hamblewood," 381, London Road, Thornton Heath.

Mr. DAVID SHARP, 2, Gresham Buildings, Basinghall Street, E.C. 2, and 7, Avonmore Road, West Kensington, W. 14.

Mr. JOHN DUDLEY FORSYTH, 51, Broadhurst Gardens, Hampstead, N.W. 6.

Mr. LEOPOLD HUBERT GEORGES WALFORD, 29, Great St. Helen's, E.C. 3.

Mr. THOMAS J. FELLOWES BROWN, "High Field," 172, Rosendale Road, West Dulwich, S.E. 21.

Mr. REGINALD JOHN PRICE, 29, Great St. Helen's, E.C. 3, and "The Hollies," Boxmoor, Herts.

Mr. HENRY ARCHIBALD CEATON, Mount Stuart Dry Docks, Ltd., Cardiff, and "Claerwen," St. Nicholas Road, Barry, Glam.

Mr. THOMAS SANDERSON HUNTER, 89, Aldgate, London, E. 1.

Mr. WILLIAM LAWRENCE HUGH JONES, 4, St. Mary Axe, Leadenhall Street, E.C. 3.

Mr. REGINALD CHARLES REED, M.A., "The Chilterns," Bourne End, Bucks, and 10, St. Catherines Road, Littlehampton, Sussex.

Mr. FREDERICK THORESBY, 1, Pump Court, Temple, E.C. 4.

Mr. FELIX SEPTIMUS BUDD, J.P., "Clarendon House," Stow Park Crescent, Newport.

Mr. ALFRED PERCY POND, 155, Fenchurch Street, E.C. 3, and "Penang," Chertsey, Surrey.

Mr. JOHN DENHOLM, Sugar Exchange, Greenock, and 155, Fenchurch Street, E.C. 3.

Mr. JAMES STANLEY ROY, 70, Gracechurch Street, London, E.C. 3, and "Menthorn," Oakwood Avenue, Purley, Surrey.

Mr. EDMUND NUTTALL, A.M.I.C.E., "Chasefield," Bowdon, Cheshire.

Mr. THOMAS LANGLEY MAYCOCK, "Hollywood," Bowdon, Cheshire.

Mr. HARRY GRAY, M.I.N.A., 89, Aldgate, London, E. 1.

Mr. FRANCIS OWEN SALISBURY, 62, Avenue Road, Regent's Park, London, N.W. 8.

SIR PERCIVAL LEE DEWHURST PERRY, K.B.E., Ewell Place, Ewell, Surrey.

Mr. WILLIAM JOHN CRAMPTON, M.I.E.E., 73, Queen Victoria Street, E.C. 4.

SIR FRANCIS HAYDN GREEN, Bart., 193, Upper Thames Street, E.C. 4, and "Inglewood House," West End Lane, N.W. 6.

Mr. EDGAR ROBERTS BROWN, 16, Upper Knollys Terrace, Plymouth, and 1, Colchester Villas, Newquay, Cornwall.

Mr. THOMAS GALLAND MELLORS, 5, Mapperly Road, Nottingham.

Alderman ALBERT BALL, J.P., 24, Wheeler Gate, Nottingham.

Lieut. GEORGE AUGUSTUS WALFORD, R. Sussex Regiment, and 50, Courtfield Gardens, Kensington, S.W. 5.

Mr. CHARLES ERNEST CLARENCE KETHRO, 136, Cromwell Road, Bristol.

Mr. TOM EDMUND LIVINGSTON OAKLEY, 40, Carey Street, Lincolns Inn, W.C. 2.

Mr. FRANK SHEARMAN, Mount Stuart Dry Docks, Ltd., Bute Docks, Cardiff, "Holme Tower," Penarth, Glam., and 10, Hanover Square, London, W. 1.

Lieut. HOWARD MAURICE EDMUNDS, M.C., Moulsecombe Place, Brighton.

Mr. WILLIAM THOMAS SYMONDS, J.P., 6, East India Avenue, London, E.C. 3., 72, Bute Street, Cardiff, and 5, Esplanade, Exmouth.

INDEX.

www.ingramcontent.com/pod-product-compliance
Lightning Source LLC
Chambersburg PA
CBHW021336290326
41933CB00038B/784